In the Tracks of the Last
STEAM TRAINS

First published by Éditions du Chêne, an imprint of Hachette-Livre
43 Quai de Grenelle, Paris 75905, Cedex 15, France
© 2000, Éditions du Chêne – Hachette-Livre
Under the title Sur les Traces des Derniers Trains à Vapeur

Editorial direction: Colette Véron
Design: Nancy Dorking
Production: Irène de Moucheron
Photo-engraving: Packédit, Paris

Language translation produced by Translate-A-Book, Oxford

© 2003, English Translation, Octopus Publishing Group Ltd, London
This edition published by Hachette Illustrated UK, Octopus Publishing Group
2–4 Heron Quays, London, E14 4JP

Printed by Tien Wah, Singapore

ISBN: 1-84430-027-7

In the Tracks of the Last
STEAM TRAINS

Cyril le Tourneur d'Ison

HACHETTE
Illustrated

Contents

To Claudine

"Every journey is a series of irreversible disappearances."

PAUL NIZAN *Aden Arabie*

"A reporter knows only one line: that of the railway."

ALBERT LONDRES

Must we look forward with dread, in the words of Paul Hamp (*Le Rail*), to "the time when railways are forgotten and lie rusting in a landscape redesigned by new inventions"?

From Guayaquil to Vladivostok, the death knell is sounding for the legendary rail lines with their obsessive rhythm that once brought people together and which left them time for their own inner journey of exploration. In these, the first years of a new millennium, in which increasingly powerful technologies continue to shrink the planet, speed has all but banished the romance and nostalgia of long-distance travel. The traveller has lost the "habit of slowness", and the mythical steam trains are drawing their last breath.

The locomotives had an alchemy that transformed water and coal into steam and flame, and the trains were redolent with "the very essence and all the magic of overland travel" (Joseph Kessel). Setting out to find those that remain in the remotest corners of the globe is to rediscover the faithful servants of a magical world, men intimately bound to the machines performing the "swan song" of the rail age. The iron road still hums to the combined music of their engines, while their lyrical solos echo on down distant valleys. This is the fabulous realm of wanderlust, of travel unbounded by time, where the ear can still catch the plaintive cries of the last iron monsters as, like mechanical vagabonds, they meander amongst the forgotten backwaters of the railway, often on narrow-gauge tracks between stations disappearing under trees.

The steam train, in whose murmuring rumble reality mingles with dream, bears witness to the still passionately living nature of a mode of transport overtaken by time. From Victor Hugo's "blind iron horse on its unyielding road" to the "raging locomotives" in which Blaise Cendrars perceives "the sobbing and wild strains of an eternal liturgy", poets have discovered a soul in these creatures: they are machines, but with the power of motion.

The clattering of the bogies and the "age-old jousting of the pistons" form the rhythmical accompaniment to comically swaying Javanese Berliners, the interminable journey across Chinese Mongolia in Spartan sleeping cars, the amazing sugar trains still wending their way across the plains of Cuba, a luxurious Rovos conquering the Zambezi, an Italian Ansaldo Breda heroically mounting the Abyssinian plateau, Resitas plunging through the forested depths of the Carpathians, the toing and froing of the excessively ornate Polish locomotives, or the epic struggles of the 779B up the Himalayan foothills.

Amongst those who forged the myths of the permanent way, the drivers are the last true Lords of the Rail, intoxicated with motion and the heady magic of depots wreathed in white steam. In the familiar and friendly bustle of the stations, travellers with no ties to bind them set off on unpredictable voyages. A snatch of conversation, a hurried glance, a whispered goodbye, a destiny about to change forever: scenes so influenced by the highly charged atmosphere of imminent departure. The leisurely course of the train dilates time and space; the journey takes on a profound significance, sharpening the traveller's perception, until the most insignificant details are dramatically revealed. Time finally registers in his memory. The landscape passes before him as if filmed by a ceaselessly panning camera, dazing him with a welter of sights and sounds, each awakening some secret recollection.

As long as the "iron road" continues to stir something inside us, then:

"Make haste, my darling,
Be afraid that one day
A train will no longer pluck at your heart."

GUILLAUME APOLLINAIRE *La Victoire*

End of a Line: The

Trans-Manchurian Express

Every day, these iron monsters set out to conquer the great Chinese north. China was the last country to build steam locomotives of any size, and today they are relegated to these northern regions. On the borders of Siberia, passenger trains still plough their way through the frozen steppes and forests of Manchuria. In Inner Mongolia, freight trains roar across lunar plateaux lashed by winds from the Gobi Desert. This is the last stand of those "raging locomotives", as Blaise Cendrars described them – before their journey to the scrapyard.

The piercing, metallic squawk of the loudspeakers echoes around the concourse of Beijing's Central Station, its never-ending monologue now and then drowned out by the cries of innumerable women selling food. A narrow corridor of metal barriers channels passengers in the right direction. People scramble madly towards the platform gates; as is the custom with China Railways, they open only 15 minutes before the train leaves. The human tide floods down the stairs; there are stampedes on the platforms, with travellers fighting their way through and taking the carriage steps by storm. In China, boarding a train has all the appearance of a mass exodus. The air that comes in through the window, laden with the pungent smells of the track ballast and the station platforms, expels the stale odours from the first-class sleepers. A blast on the guard's whistle. Buffers crash against each other, the unwilling, massive carriages creak, there are sudden vibrations from the rails ... and the long-distance for Harbin lurches into motion.

RIGHT:
A large proportion of China Railways' employees are women. Frequently authoritarian, they ensure the network runs efficiently.

FAR RIGHT:
Control room in a small station north of Nancha, a few miles from the Russian border.

The express slips away through the entrails of the old imperial city before threading its way along the first frozen tracks streaked with white. A few puny, stark trees fly past in a still indeterminate landscape – Mongolia begins at the gates of Beijing. In the second-class sleeper, where there are no corridors or doors, only a kind of dormitory with superimposed bunks, people begin to organise themselves. An old woman in a garment of padded rags has already found customers for her "hundred-year-old-eggs" (preserved for three months in a mixture of clay and straw) and her spicy noodles. The train is inundated with food. Sunflower seeds, fish bones, duck bones – the floor swiftly disappears under the debris. Boisterous card games fail to disturb the calm mah jong players. A passenger clad in a sort of greenish pyjama suit clears a way between bed linen hanging from the bunks, alternately puffing on his cigarette and spitting.

Back in the relative solitude of first-class, there is still no escape from the bellowing radio. A vestige of the propaganda system, revolutionary chants are interspersed with readings from slushy novels. Noisily clearing their throats in turn, our fellow passengers in this compartment swig a last mouthful of tea; in China, travellers never part with their old jam jar half-filled with sodden tea leaves, which they reuse ad infinitum. A concert of snores breaks out in the sleeper as it rocks to the rhythm of the rails, the occasional brief crescendo drowning out the rumbling of the wheels.

Five hundred and twenty-eight miles (850 km) later, in a bluish halo of frost, the outlines of a forest of industrial chimneys loom up through the smog. Shenyang, ancient Mukden, is a typical, nightmarish Chinese megalopolis. From the outskirts to the centre, countless factories dominate this city of four million inhabitants. We see their frozen faces, their cautious steps on the icy asphalt – muffled-up silhouettes treated with contempt by the ceaseless flood of battle-hardened cyclists ...

We take a look round Shenyang station before boarding our connection for Harbin: express No. 317. A train whistle shrieks; far away, the platform bridge is enveloped in clouds of white steam that billow and swirl up among the iron roof beams. Apparently unaffected by this dripping fog, passengers continue on their way, leaving a ghostly wake. The powerful engine

snorts out a second deafening jet of steam. Another engine replies, demanding right of precedence. The conversation-like exchange of whistles and the swirling vapour magically transform the station approaches, hiding the sinister effect of the district's washed-out facades.

Of the few remaining steam train depots, Sujiatun, near Shenyang, undoubtedly offers the most impressive spectacle. The last Chinese-built steam engine was produced at the Datong factory in 1989, and a score of such loco-motives is on parade each day, the most up to date being the Qian Jin 2-10-2 – the name means "Onward!" – the Shan Yan 2-8-2 ("Climb Higher!") and the Shangyou 2-6-2 ("Swim against the Tide!"). Blackened with soot, this vast depot is the sanctuary of every *huoche* (literally, fire-carriage) in northern China. Under its tall windows, grey with dust, and giant canopy lie the

maintenance workshops, situated at the locomotives' "bedsides". Men and women fitters busy themselves around these sleeping monsters, whose metal carapaces gleam with unreal reflections. Strange pulsating noises emanate from the tangled maze of pipes, despite the apparently torpid state of the machinery. Spasmodic breathing, sometimes erupting in a gasp, and expiring in brief squeaks or plaintive groans, reveals there is still life in these creatures of iron and fire.

The doors of an engine shed are opened, and spurts of steam emerge as a Qian Jin (QJ) 2-10-2, its wheels repainted bright red, departs after its compulsory three-day service. The locomotive shudders, seemingly hesitating at the sight of the confusing web of rails. Blowing off a burst of steam to reassure itself, it boldly moves forward into the labyrinth, clattering across the tracks with a noise like muffled cymbals.

A little further off, along the embankment, old women are picking up pieces of coal fallen from the mineral trains; they fill wicker baskets with this precious fuel to heat their houses.

Leaving the interminable, grey suburbs of Shenyang, the express gradually regains cruising speed. The trees seem to be dashing along the embankment, while the contours of the horizon rush to meet us. At the foot of dark, bare hills we spot the smoking chimneys of houses in a

village, all huddled together under a leaden sky. A freezing mist drifts over the cracked fields beyond. In the north of Liaoning Province, the countryside has a look of desolation. "No one knows where God placed Paradise, but it certainly isn't here," wrote a French missionary passing through the territory in 1846. Earlier visitors were the hordes of Mongolian horsemen who bore down upon this vast, flat region to overthrow the Ming dynasty in 1644.

Near the Fushun complex, which boasts the largest open mine in China, a Pacific Class SL with 12 bogies hurtles by, making our compartment windows rattle. Then our train plunges a little further into the Great North, formerly Manchuria, in the freezing grip of winter. Icicles have formed around the vestibules that link the carriages. The corridor is encrusted with frozen spittle and the temperature is down to zero in the restaurant car. A crimson-faced Manchurian opium addict, wearing a *chapka* and a green military overcoat, is sipping away at some sort of fantastic pick-me-up based on glutinous rice alcohol. In the second-class sleeper, heating is virtually non-existent: Maoist doctrine classed it as a luxury.

At Changchun – the name, somewhat absurdly, means "Eternal Spring" – the rails are covered in snow. Once the capital of the Japanese puppet state of Manchukuo, it marked the junction between the Russian and Japanese rail systems. The Trans-Manchurian was completed in 1901 as part of the Trans-Siberian Railway, built by the tsars to connect Moscow with ports on the Pacific. After the crushing defeat of the Russians by the Japanese in 1905, this section was replaced by alternative routes. The Trans-Manchurian fell into first Chinese, then Japanese hands. In 1945, the Soviet Union occupied Manchuria and retained control of the railway (which the Japanese had modernised) until 1953, when it was restored to China, by now under the control of Mao. Today, besides carrying regional traffic, it remains one of several "Trans-Siberian" routes to the Far East. From Moscow to Beijing (a week's travel) the distance is 5,625 miles (9,001 km).

At Changchun station, alive with locomotives in steam, there is a warm welcome. Constructed between 1934 and 1936, two Japanese engines in perfect working order are being fired up in the engine sheds, garlands of icicles hanging from their cabs. A cleaner has just emptied the ashbox and the glowing embers are burning themselves out between the rails: a study in ice and fire amid clouds of white steam dispersed in the wind like cotton wool. Snowflakes lodge in the driver's hair; eyes fixed on the pressure gauge, he opens the

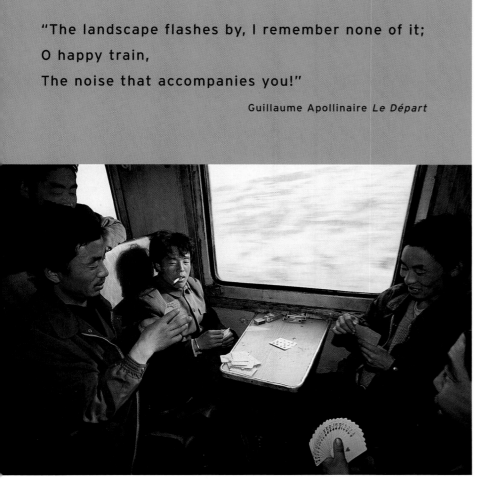

"The landscape flashes by, I remember none of it;
O happy train,
The noise that accompanies you!"

Guillaume Apollinaire *Le Départ*

cylinder cocks and the regulator. A headlamp is illuminated, and needles of frost sparkle in its light. At his window, the fireman adjusts his threadbare cap. Slowly, almost imperceptibly, the connecting rods come to life, transmitting their movement to the ten driven wheels with their red rims. As the pressure rises, the boiler begins to roar; shovelfuls of coal are thrust again and again in ever quickening succession into the red-hot firebox, even though the wheels keep slithering on the frozen rails. This, according to Blaise Cendrars, is the moment when "the locomotive bellows with overheated fury".

LEFT: Whilst the frozen landscape of Manchuria unravels as if filmed by a ceaselessly panning camera, boisterous card games take place in second-class.

Sporting a uniform recalling that of the Red Guards, the woman ticket inspector on our train laughs bizarrely as she indulges in an exchange with a passenger – a surveyor, judging by his graphometer and clumsy tripod. The lady in question, impressively built and inflexible in matters of discipline, is using that notorious Chinese laugh – which rarely expresses a reaction to something amusing – to dislodge this unfortunate individual who has ensconced himself in a first-class seat without the necessary ticket. On Chinese railways, women rule the roost.

At distant Harbin, famous for its Festival of Ice Lanterns and the quality of its ginseng, the temperature has tumbled to –31°F (–35°C). The frozen waters of the Black Dragon river bisect this city, the capital of Heilonjiang Province ("Kingdom of the Rats"), before meandering through Russia, where it becomes the Amur.

From Harbin, we take an unheated stopping train and travel the 118 miles (190 km) southeast along the old Vladivostok route to the little station of Weihe. There, another change is required for the essential excursion through one of the last great forests and wildlife refuges in northern China. On the platform at Weihe, a passing forestry train whips up a whirlwind of ice crystals as sharp as needles. The narrow-gauge Weihe Forestry Railway branch is shared by

passenger and loggers' trains and threads its way between hills that appear blue from the intense cold, before plunging into a forest of conifers. Its destiny is inextricably linked to the mass-production of furniture, chopsticks, toothpicks, and the like. In this country, prosperity goes hand in hand with deforestation and pollution. As for the fate of wildlife, one only has to glance at the restaurant menus in Harbin or Shenyang – grilled bear's paws and all sorts of rare birds – to realise how, for the Chinese in such matters, the stomach rules the heart.

Zhenzhu, Xinli, Xiping, Pinglin ... one by one, our train leaves these Lilliputian halts in its wake, all of them inaccessible by road in their forest isolation. Xinli is reminiscent of the Wild West. A few red lanterns glow through the blizzard. The only living creatures are a logger, his sled piled high with timber, and his horse. Manchuria was taken over by the Han, but this old man is an authentic Manchurian, with immense forehead, projecting cheekbones, flesh sculpted and wrinkled by the bitter cold. The ear protectors of his *chapka* flap in the wind like a bird's wings. On a cracked wall, yellowing characters recall the good old days of propaganda slogans: "The people's railway is for the people."

Back to Harbin to catch express No. 209, which is about to leave. We are now beginning a long trek to another distant point: Baotou, the Yellow River, and the Gobi Desert. The train races south through darkness rent by lightning. The first-class sleeper is brand new. Parked like rows of onions on the pink carpet, comfortable slippers await the traveller; they are made of plastic and bear the logo of a famous American sports shoe manufacturer. The arrival of night has concealed the change in the landscape: behind the turquoise curtains of the compartment stretch out the jagged, ochre plateaux of Mongolia.

To the accompaniment of lively music from the loudspeakers, the official in charge of the carriage (a woman) organises a communal keep-fit session in the corridor. For foreigners travelling independently, reaching the sublime Reshui valley requires determination and the patience of Job when dealing with the local authorities. It is not long since this region was inaccessible to non-Chinese. Between Tongliao and Linxi, the ancient locomotives accomplish daily miracles. Here, the beauty of nature takes one's breath away; as far as rail journeys are concerned, there is nothing to match this for sheer poetry.

After leaving Tongliao, the passenger train begins an inexorable ascent of the mountainside, the panting of the engines echoing like a giant's among the rocky slopes. Pulled by two QJ

2-10-2s – yes, 20 driving wheels in all – the train seems to pierce the mountain, struggling ever higher, turning back on itself, twisting endlessly, and finally plunging into the blackness of a tunnel. A short silence, then a growl emerges from inside the mountain, and it reappears shrieking on the other side. Smoke billows by the windows before swirling high up to cover the sky like a white shroud. As we climb the mountainsides, bathed in icy, blue shadow, the gasping of the cylinders is muffled by the deep

ABOVE:
Day's end near the Manchurian border: a railway worker heads for home. "Like gilded plaits of horsehair, the rails ran away in front of us." Jules Romains *Lucienne*.

snow lying on the terraces. Gathering all their mechanical might, the locomotives finally sweep down to the viaduct over the Reshui valley, a surreal-looking piece of engineering suspended in the immense void above the adobe dwellings of Mongolian peasants.

In days gone by, the Chinese called this the Gate of the Demons; the Gobi Desert and its howling winds inspired them with deep terror. South of Baotou, another disfigured Chinese city of Inner Mongolia, a line 37 miles (60 km) long takes us through a lunar landscape, which marks the transition to the Gobi. This is the route linking Baotou and Dongsheng, a town struggling to shake itself free from the sinister, blackened plain that begins just outside the city. Here, coal is the absolute monarch. Flurries of slag are thrown up behind the interminable truck convoys. The wizened trees, fields strewn with clinker, a denuded countryside: these are the unavoidable results of China's cultural obsession with the total domination of nature by man.

By an ice-bound river, reddish cliffs rise up at last to meet the train. On the opposite bank lie the mythical "Singing Sands". Legend tells how there once existed a Buddhist temple on what is now a sea of dunes. The lamas rashly cut down every living tree and the sands took their place, eventually swallowing up temple and lamas alike. Ever since, they say that when the winds rage down among the dunes one can hear the lamas chanting. A tale modern China would do well to meditate upon more often.

ABOVE: The driver sounds the whistle and weird noises as if from muffled cymbals begin to rise from the pistons.
BELOW: The concourse of Nancha station in the early morning: a happy Manchurian traveller.

Above: Clouds of steam and an exchange of whistles magically transform Shenyang station, where about ten locomotives are still in perfect working order. Below: In the half-light of the engine sheds, a maintenance man cleans the connecting rods.

"As we drew near Mongolia
Which roared like a blazing building,
The train slowed its pace,
And I perceived in the interminable squealing of its wheels
The sobbing and wild strains of an eternal liturgy."

Blaise Cendrars *Du monde entier*

BELOW, LEFT:
At –22°F (–30°C),
any water
leaking from
the locomotive
freezes in
moments.
Garlands of
icicles hang
from the cabs.

BELOW, RIGHT:
An army of
mechanics
swarms over
the engines
at Shenyang.

OPPOSITE PAGE:
Railway worker
silhouetted on a
Changchun
platform.
Everything is in
black and white in
this strange and
unreal world.

LEFT: Nancha
station: on the
Chinese network,
stations are
meticulously
maintained.

ABOVE:
In the great
Chinese north,
these iron
monsters plough
their way across
some 350,000
square miles
(900,000 km²)
of ice and snow.
With
temperatures
below −22°F
(−30°C), the
engines leave a
ghostly wake
behind them.

OVERLEAF:
In the Reshui
valley (Inner
Mongolia),
between the
snowbound
terraces, the
train "passed
with the
violence of
a storm, as
if sweeping
everything
before it."
Émile Zola
*La Bête
humaine*.

RIGHT:
On the platform of a small, deserted halt, a single peasant awaits his train. In the background, the jagged plateaux of Chinese Mongolia.

OPPOSITE PAGE, BOTTOM RIGHT: The Yabuli forestry line runs through the main streets of Manchurian villages inaccessible by road during the winter.

BOTTOM LEFT:
Frontage of a restaurant in Nancha, the railway capital of China's extreme north, in the distant province of Heilonjiang.

BOTTOM RIGHT:
A Mongolian horseman gives way to an express pulled by two locomotives.

ABOVE: Passenger train after descending the barren slopes of the Mongolian plateau; the guard checks the platform before continuing.
BELOW: The depot at Changchun, capital of Jilin Province, the last area in China to have hundreds of steam locomotives still in service.

ABOVE: At Changchun, together with Shenyang the last sanctuary for steam locomotives, dismantling has already begun.
BELOW: Loud panting noises emanate from the boiler. "The locomotive bellows with overheated fury." Blaise Cendrars *Du monde entier*.

PRECEDING PAGES: South of Baotou, passenger trains skirt the Gobi Desert.

ABOVE: "It could be heard emerging from the tunnel and panting more noisily in the open country. Then it roared by in a thunder of wheels and massive wagons, with all the invincible power of a hurricane." Émile Zola *La Bête humaine.*

OPPOSITE PAGE: In the heart of Chinese Mongolia, between Tongliao and Linxi, ancient locomotives perform miracles. Interminable trains struggle daily up the Jingpeng Pass before descending the sublime slopes of the Reshui valley. (At the end of the nineteenth century, Imperial Russia constructed the Trans-Manchurian Railway. In northern China, parts of the infrastructure were built under the Russian or Japanese occupations.)

PRECEDING PAGES:
A QJ 2-10-2 has just managed to escape from snowbound Changchun station. Everything was blotted out by "the roar of the engine opening its cylinder cocks and blowing off whirlwinds of white steam." Émile Zola *La Bête humaine*.

OPPOSITE PAGE:
Logo of the Chinese rail system on Nancha station. Steam trains were scheduled to disappear from regular routes in China during 2001.

TOP:
Immense frozen wastes extend from northern Manchuria to the edge of the Gobi in the south.

BOTTOM:
One of the last "raging locomotives" to set the earth quaking with its iron thunder and shrieking whistle.

OVERLEAF:
A train surges over the Jingpeng Pass amid the rugged plateaux of Mongolia.

Cuba: The Sugar Trains

etween the coffee plantations of Cuba's Oriente Mountains and the tobacco fields of the western hills extend the battle lines of the *zafra* or sugar harvest, an immense, verdant plain seething with activity from December to mid-June. On this Caribbean island, the harvest is to all intents and purposes a real war with its own weapons and shock troops. Day and night, a railway, unique in the whole world, transports the precious sugar cane from one end of the island to the other. For 40 years, the heroes of the Revolution have been cutting cane with machetes, and more than 100 antiquated locomotives shuttle through the plantations, bringing the crop and its nectar to the sugar mills or *centrales.*

Con sangre se hace azúcar. "Sugar is made with blood". Such is the saying passed down in the industry from generation to generation. It first appeared on the plantations themselves and is a reminder of the brutal colonial past, a history inseparable from the great sugar-trading saga that began in 1523 and still dominates the life of this big Antillan island. The earliest rail line in Latin America was constructed here in 1838 to transport the cane crop. The epic partnership between rail and sugar originated just outside the town of Trinidad, by popular consent the jewel of the Caribbean, where a 12.5-mile (20-km) track was constructed through the valley of Los Ingenios, also known as the Valle de San Luis. This valley contains miles and miles of cane fields stretching to the

horizon in a sea of intense green, with here and there a scattering of royal palms: a kind of forgotten El Dorado in its exquisite mountain setting. Here, in the eighteenth century, in the 50 *ingenios* that processed the valley's crop, the slaves endured a living hell. On every plantation, bent nearly double, they toiled for 16 hours a day, their routine controlled by the regular tolling of a bell. The tower of Sanchez Iznaga stands as a witness to those times; some 150 ft (45 m) above the ocean of cane, it served both as a belfry and a guard platform.

Not far distant, dwarfed by the immense cane plants sometimes reaching 23 ft (7 m), José Leonardo Marin whirls his machete with incredible dexterity, his arm describing lightning-swift arcs against the sky. Armful after armful, he aims to cut the plant at the base, where the concentration of sucrose is highest. His skin is plastered with sugary sap and sweat. His fellow *macheteros* are way behind him. The line of men has been staggered at the start of the field according to their cutting speed to stop them getting in each other's way. But already, heaps weighing 6–8 cwt (300–400 kg) are piling up behind José Marin. Each worker's harvest is loaded into individual trailers; at night, in the dormitory block, the inspector compares the tallies. José Marin has nothing to fear: he is the best of the 45 *macheteros* of the 5th Party Congress Brigade. At 31, he is a *supermachetero* and a *millionario*, meaning he has already cut more than a million *arrobas* of cane. With each *arroba* weighing just over 25 lb (11.5 kg), this is more than 11,000 tons! Here is a millionaire, Cuban-style, or what they used to call in the Soviet Union a "Stakhanovite": someone constantly dedicated to outdoing his own previous production record. During the previous *zafra*, he averaged more than a thousand *arrobas* a day on his own; most cutters manage about 400.

Sugar workers usually have nicknames, sometimes humorous, sometimes heroic. José's workmates call him El Madrugador ("The Early One"), as he makes a habit of "not waiting for the cock to crow before getting up, and he arrives in the fields well before his *campañeros* in the Brigade". For 40 years, the regime of the "Lider Maximo", Fidel Castro, has continued to motivate the *macheteros*, spearhead of the Revolution, with a system of rewards

The Raoul Sanchez Brigade is one of the best in Cuba. Famous for its productivity records, it can field 50 *macheteros* "willing to work their hearts out", boasts the Party secretary and Brigade chief.

and payments in kind. Following in his father's footsteps – he was three times made a "Hero of Labour of the Republic of Cuba" – José has already won ten medals, thirteen bicycles, five cooling fans, a Lada car and, in 1999, a trip to Paris.

The day ends for the 5th Party Congress Brigade. Exhausted, the cutters pile into a trailer to be driven back to camp. In the distance, behind the tall thickets of swaying cane, the huge chimney of the Pepito Tey sugar mill is belching out a whitish smoke as it prepares to crush the harvest of four brigades of *macheteros*. Night has already fallen when the puffing of the Baldwin locomotives comes into earshot. Whistle answers whistle; headlamps shoot bluish fingers of light towards the ash-grey horizon. Under this veil of darkness, fantastical jets of steam dissolve into "tiny wisps of vapour, scattering themselves like white tears on the infinite mourning robe of the sky."[1] The cane wagons pile up in the *patio* (yard) of the mill. Already, the "Lords of the Rails" – the drivers – have taken over from the "Lords of the Machete". Their task is to convey the enormous quantity of cane to the mill before it spoils.

Mostly, the sugar mills bear the name of a martyr of the Revolution. But before becoming Pepito Tey – the name of a combatant who fell gloriously during the uprising in Santiago de Cuba – the present factory was the Soledad del Muerto or "Solitude of Death", after a former owner, the Marquis Dominguo de Sania. He was a specimen of the *sacarocracia*, or Creole sugar aristocracy, of the period. At the conclusion of each harvest, his custom was to disappear with three slaves and bury the proceeds of the *zafra* in some secret place. The loot safely hidden, he would habitually kill all three slaves. This went on year after year.

Later, this mill was one of the first to attract the attentions of the Americans because of its proximity to the port of Cienfuegos.

From the second half of the nineteenth century, American locomotives arrived by the dozen in Cuba, rails were shipped through the Panama Canal, and the "white gold" of the Caribbean fell into the hands of Uncle Sam. At the time of the outbreak of the Castro Revolution in 1953, cane plantations made up 80 per cent of land under cultivation, and of the 22 major estates, 13 were American-owned. United Fruit reigned over more than 250,000 acres (100,000 ha) in Cuba. Whether black or white, *macheteros* or rail workers, the struggling sugar workers at Pepito Tey were among the first to take up the cry of *Cuba Libre*. Later, well after the "triumph of the Revolution" in 1959, the country's fate remained bound up with the sugar harvest. Strangled by the American embargo, the island was condemned to live using the technology of the machete and the steam engine. Castro could hardly refuse when the Soviet Union offered to trade oil and machinery for Cuban sugar.

In order to find the manager's office in the labyrinth of a sugar mill, one has only to look for a building equipped with air-conditioning. At the Manuel de Cespedes mill (named after a *libertador* or hero of the first struggle for independence in 1868), a secretary is reading Pablo Neruda's *Twenty Poems of Love and a Song of Despair*. Whilst waiting for the director, she declaims aloud poem No. 20, while images of Che and Fidel gaze down from yellowing portraits on the peeling walls of the colonial building. When she gets up to call the rail manager, "her body undulates like paper made from bagasse" (Zoe Valdes).

The smell of molasses is absent from the pleasantly cool office of Comrade Director as he gives us an optimistic summary of this year's *zafra*. Zoe Valdes' vitriolic pen would have protested: "We were told we must harvest gigantic *zafras*, sacrifice everything down to the last drop of our blood, drown ourselves in the sea if necessary. The *zafras* disappeared under a mountain of propaganda."

Cuba possesses a formidable transport advantage, with a rail network that is the densest in Latin America. When railways were established on the island in the mid-1800s, each mill had its

own lines to collect cane and transport sugar to the nearest port. As a result, numerous companies led a prosperous existence until the late 1930s, with already more than 3,000 miles (5,000 km) of track devoted to passenger traffic and around 6,250 miles (10,000 km) of lines for the sugar industry. Today, the latter total 4,811 miles (7,742 km) – 65 per cent

of which is standard-gauge track – and serve a hundred or so of the 154 mills. Of the 300-odd old locomotives on the island, around a hundred remain in working order. For the most part these are ancient American Baldwin 0-6-0s, constructed between 1910 and 1930; despite being constantly patched up, they continue to manoeuvre the cage-like cane wagons with sall their old panache.

Ernesto Diaz, nicknamed El Sapito ("Little Frog"), is the driver of a magnificent 1916 Baldwin; her livery is freshly repainted, with red stripes running along above the bogies, and the headboard sports the slogan *Venceremos* ("We will be victorious") surrounded with white stars. El Sapito's hand firmly grips the oil-flow valve – 90 per cent of Cuban steam locomotives use oil-fired boilers. This one is pulling some 40 wagons piled high with sugar cane and the crew strive

for every ounce of power to make the last gradient to the mill. Short of breath, the 22 cylinders start to pant, before regaining their self-confidence and pounding out the cymbal-like rhythm known as the "bossa nova of the rails". El Sapito beams a broad smile: not for anything would he drive a diesel. An immense, black cloud boils up in the locomotive's wake, high above the tops of the silk-cotton trees. With a deafening roar, flames leap from the firebox and a tremulous rumble comes from underfoot.

On the foothills of Pinar del Rio, at the approach to the Boris Luis Colona mill, an enormous slogan screams to the *macheteros*: *Azucareros a la vanguardia!* ("Sugar workers to the vanguard!"). Unfortunately for the Revolution, the heroic image of the struggling sugar worker has definitely lost its appeal. Amongst the young, there is no great rush to sign up for the "sugar front". In the valley regions, sugar cane is under sentence of death. Such is the decision of the Lider Maximo. What is to become of what Erik Orsenna called "this inland sea which feeds the whole of Cuba"?

---

1. Émile Zola *La Bête humaine.*

Opposite: A maintenance worker extricating himself from the boiler of a Baldwin. Above: In the workshops of the Cuba Libre mill, a welder strikes a typical Cuban pose. Below: Young driver checking the wagons; they jolt about on the tracks and when overloaded can often derail.

ABOVE:
There are still over a hundred steam locomotives functioning on the island. Most are American, the rest German.

RIGHT:
Clinging to the whistle of his locomotive, a driver attempts to clear the tracks, which are repeatedly blocked at the approach to villages.

FAR RIGHT:
Young driver checking the wagons; they jolt about on the tracks and when overloaded can often derail. Like their comrades, the *macheteros*, whose mythical status in the Revolution is perpetuated by the State, the "Lords of the Rails" have their special place in the caste system of Cuban workers.

ABOVE AND RIGHT:
A champion
cane-cutter,
José Leonardo
Marin has won
numerous awards
for his skill and
productivity.

OPPOSITE PAGE,
BOTTOM RIGHT:
José's comrade
Manuel.
These two
"super-cutters"
have worked in
the most
prestigious
brigades of
macheteros.
José has beaten
all the records,
and has been
made a Hero
of Labour of
the Republic
of Cuba.

OVERLEAF:
Manuel,
a virtuoso in
mid-performance.

52

CERTIFICADO
MEJOR MACHETERO
DEL MUNICIPIO

End of the day
for the 5th Party
Congress Brigade.
The *macheteros*
start at 6.30 am;
by sunset they
are required to
have cut a
quantity of cane
previously fixed
by the Brigade
chief.

ABOVE AND RIGHT:
The first rail line
in Latin America
was constructed
in Cuba in 1838
to transport the
cane harvest.
The demands of
the sugar
companies made
the network the
densest in the
Americas by the
start of the
1900s.

In Cuba more than anywhere else, the passage
of trains is reminiscent of rhythmical music.
"Like the beat of clattering cymbals, the 'bossa
nova of rails wedded to sleepers [crossties]'
keeps time with the panting cylinders."

Jacques Réda *Hors les murs*

BELOW:
Entrance to the Boris Luis Santa Colona, one of the mills nearest to Havana. Now regarded as part of the "agro-industrial complex", most of them date from the second half of the nineteenth century.

OPPOSITE PAGE, BOTTOM:
The director's son and his friend show off a dazzling 1954 Buick outside Hermanos Ameijeiras.

PRECEDING PAGES:
A locomotive from the Hermanos Ameijeiras mill passing through the village of Zulueta.

RIGHT:
The armada of Baldwin 0-6-0s at the Gregorio Malaica mill.

OVERLEAF:
In the northwest of the island, a Baldwin returns to the depot with the day's last load.

Eritrea: The

Resurrection of a Railway

Nine years after the end of the struggle for independence from Ethiopia, Eritrea's colonial railway is slowly being reborn from its ashes. Former rebels have turned themselves into navvies to reconstruct the spectacular Red Sea line. With the help of retired rail workers, and despite recurrent spats with Big Brother Ethiopia, Eritrea is re-enacting the engineering triumph achieved by the Italians in 1911.

One morning in September 1975, an Ansaldo Breda steam locomotive fought its way up to the Abyssinian plateau 7,856 ft (2,394 m) above the shores of the Red Sea. Clanking and clattering, it passed through the maze of tracks outside the station at Asmara, Eritrea's capital, then under Ethiopian occupation. The 400 passengers were unaware of the importance of the occasion; it was in fact the last journey of the Red Sea Train. The war of independence with Ethiopia sounded the death knell for one of the world's most astonishing railways.

The Eritrean rising against Ethiopian domination began in September 1961 during the reign of the Negus, Emperor Haile Selassie. The struggle intensified with the establishment of Marxism in Ethiopia under the "Red Negus", Colonel Mengistu. During these long years of warfare, the rail network was partly destroyed by the Ethiopians, partly dismantled by the guerrillas of the Eritrean People's Liberation Front (EPLF), who used railway materials to strengthen trenches and bunkers. During the 1980s, countless assaults were launched by Mengistu against the Eritrean heights, only for them to be smashed by the rebel forces. In May 1991, the "tattered forces of the former Red Negus, staring

PRECEDING PAGES: Track worker near Damas.

OPPOSITE: Before its destruction, Eritrea's rail system covered nearly 190 miles (300 km), extending from the shores of the Red Sea to Akordat on the northern edge of the high plateau, towards the Sudanese border. Little by little, the Eritreans are reconstructing their railway, recovering sections of track used by the EPLF to make bunkers.

ABOVE:
Ghinda station,
recently
reconstructed, is
gradually
coming back to
life. Trains now
run again
between this
little town,
huddled at the
foot of the
escarpment, and
Massawa on the
shores of the
Red Sea.

blank-faced at defeat, rejected by History"[1], evacuated Eritrea. By the end of the war of independence, which had lasted 30 years, Eritrea's railway – "the history of colonialism in a nutshell"[2] – was reduced to scrap.

From 1887 to 1911, the then colonial power, Italy, established the basic framework of this highly "acrobatic" route. At almost exactly the same time (1897–1917), the French were building the line from Djibouti to Addis Ababa, and contemporary colonial propaganda suggested that this was a competition between the Italian engineers and their French counterparts. But in the context of twentieth-century industrial history, the railway of the *bersaglieri* stands out as a real triumph of engineering. Along the vertiginous escarpment which climbs for 73 miles (117 km) from the Red Sea to Asmara, there are 30 tunnels and more than 60 bridges or viaducts, with gradients that sometimes reach as much as 35 per mill. Before its destruction, the line was about 190 miles (300 km) long, terminating at the town of Akordat, on the northern edges of the high plateau, towards the border with Sudan.

In the mid-1930s, at the height of rail activity, over 30 trains worked the line each day. Travellers from the Red Sea boarded the train at Massawa, a port that seems to hover between sea and sky, one of those great cities of Eastern legend, with the white edges of its buildings etched against a sea dark as ink. In its Turkish-Egyptian setting, isolated at the far end of a causeway, the city had a panoramic view of the locomotives coursing proudly along the isthmus. Its Moorish arcades witnessed the arrival of many a famous traveller bewitched by the Horn of Africa, from Arthur Rimbaud to Henri de Monfried. Massawa, an outpost on the enchanting shores of the Red Sea, saw all of Rimbaud's sons fall under the spell of what Romain Gary described as "the unique magic of the place". In a mist of nostalgia, they set out to taste the triumphs and the tragedies of the Queen of Sheba's descendants.

In the burning desert, the life of little towns like Mai Atal, Damas or Baresa was regulated by the whistles of the locomotives. Further on, the train stopped at Ghinda. Here passengers enjoyed a delicious respite, a cool oasis between the fiery shores of the Horn and the lush foothills of the Abyssinian plateau. Every ethnic group, Tigre, Tigrinya, Afar, and others, met in the shade of the little station's arcades, under the Italian-style pergolas swarming with delicate purple flowers. After taking in the last views while the train teetered on the edge of the void, the seven-hour journey ended at Asmara. Leaving the station, the traveller was greeted by avenues bordered with palm trees and hollyhocks. The metamorphosis was completed by interminable café terraces and lines of Tuscan or Piedmontese facades sculpted in a kind of bas-relief by the intense shadows.

Shortly after Eritrea's declaration of independence (25 May 1993), the government of President Issaias Afwerki took what seemed a crazy decision: to rebuild the colonial rail line as an

> "It was one of those locomotives with twin coupled axles, enormous but graceful and elegant, with its great, lightweight wheels linked by steel arms, its broad chest, its sweeping, powerful flanks, all the logic and all the certainty which make up the incomparable beauty of the machine: a combination of strength and precision."
>
> Émile Zola *La Bête humaine*

exact replica. The infant Eritrean state now launched a new general mobilization. The extraordinary capacity for organization that had served the guerrillas so well during the war rallied again to this outrageous project. More than 50 veteran rail workers answered the government's appeal – every one of them had learned his trade under the Italian colonial administration, and their average age was 70. Their task was to restore to working order the Ansaldo steam locomotives and the Fiat *Littorina* railcars. For more than 20 years, these iron monsters had languished in the depot at Asmara, overgrown with brambles.

Today, the programme for Eritrea's reconstruction involves compulsory national service, mobilizing men and women, peasants and students alike for the restoration of the rail system. An immense collection of railway material has been put together throughout the country. Ex-combatants have turned railwaymen. Again they mount an assault on the hilltops – but this time to recover rails and other items once taken from the railway and hauled up there to build defences. From every hill, every headland, they bring down piles of rusted metal. Then begins a meticulous reconstruction, yard by yard; a process which says much for the energy and determination of the Eritreans.

In 1995, Italy and the United States offered to construct a new, standard-gauge line equipped with modern rolling stock. The Eritrean government declined all such offers of foreign aid. When they first built this railway, the Italians were unaware that they were helping to forge the Eritrean nation; for this tiny country of three and a half million inhabitants with its colourful colonial past, the railway has become a symbol not merely of development but also of its sovereignty. Among Eritrea's reconstruction projects, the Red Sea line is undoubtedly the one that most clearly reflects the nation's pride.

Around the small town of Ghinda, halfway between the Red Sea and the high plateau, the rain is cascading down. Brief moments of light allow a glimpse of the sky above the darkened hills. As night dissolves into day, a few dozen track workers say goodbye to their families camped

ABOVE: This youngster of 74 is acquainted with the smallest cog in the 1932 Ansaldo Breda he has been tending for months on end. It will still be years before the railway is completely restored and his locomotive can once more roar down the hill towards the Red Sea.

71

in tents among the clumps of acacias. Wrapped in the traditional *chamma*, they march through the mud with arms crossed and sticks across their shoulders to the work site at kilometre 82. As the line advances, the camp also moves, taking with it the tents for the forges in which bolts and clips are refashioned.

Standing at the base of a cliff where a rock fall has taken place, two veteran foremen, Idriss (65) and Tagai (70), wait for their gang. Idriss supervises the laying of the sleepers (crossties). Carefully checking the alignment, he decides the future path of the track and ensures the sleepers are approximately 2 ft 4 in (0.70 m) apart. The terrain has been furrowed by the rains, making track-laying difficult. Eight men are required to lay a section of rail 29 ft 6 in (9 m) long and weighing nearly 5 cwt (250 kg). (The ballast and fastenings are added later.) The line advances on average around 300 yards (275 m) a day. As they approach the mountain, the intended path begins to curve, forcing the workers to bend the rails. The method used is an outdated one: it gives the required degree of curvature, but it involves a back-breaking struggle.

The tops of the eucalyptus trees bordering the track turn to flame in the sunlight. Eighteen or so miles (30 km) lower down the track, where the winds from the Red Sea set the thorn bushes trembling, two hundred men are fixing the rails to the sleepers and spreading ballast. An Afar foreman with huge, shining eyes patrols the line, checking the rails with his level.

A Russian Ural truck – captured from the Ethiopians during the war – has been mounted on a bogie and is used to test the track and to bring ballast up to the work site. But at Damas, a small village littered with the carcasses of disembowelled wagons, the torrential rainfall has carried away a bridge, leaving the rails miraculously suspended. It is too dangerous for the half-truck, half-train to proceed. The whole village then turns out to help the track workers bridge the gaping hole.

At Asmara, the mists have enveloped the *ferrovia*, the old station way up in its eyrie nearly 8,000 ft (2,400 m) above sea level. Remains of the tracks, battered out of shape during the conflict, add a ghostly air to the station approaches. In the workshops, 25 white-haired railwaymen attempt the impossible: to being back to life six steam locomotives and as many diesels, all of Italian origin. All the workers at Asmara are old-timers. They are the memory bank of the Eritrean railway, the only ones still able to speak fluently the language of cylinders and pistons. They all worked on the railway's locomotives during the years 1930 to 1950; all evince the same joy at the idea of resurrecting a technology that shaped their youth. Their movements

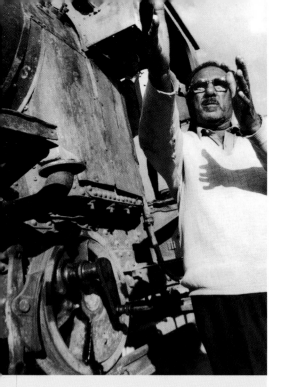

In reconstructing its railway, Eritrea has defied the world by declining all outside aid, placing its faith in its own resources.

may be slow, but a twinkle in their eyes indicates the clarity of mind with which they can appraise a problem.

At 72, Teka Taggai, a specialist in locomotive instrumentation, was among the first volunteers to respond to the government's appeal. For him, nothing has altered about the technology of steam pressure gauges. He pays homage to the British for the training he received while they administered Eritrea during the 1940s, but begrudges the fact that they spirited away four steam locomotives and sent them to India. During the period of their occupation (1941–52), the British had no qualms about depriving the country of a funicular railway 50 miles (80 km) long, as well as of most of the factories built by the Italians.

Seyoum Beraki, wearing blue overalls with patches all over them and a baseball cap perched crookedly on his head, becomes ecstatic as soon as conversation turns to the three Ansaldo steam locomotives now working as well as ever. He is 75, and the oldest of the team. He makes no attempt to conceal his passion for the locomotive he fusses over from morning to night. "She could go on for another 50 years," he declares, straightening his cap. But what everyone is eagerly awaiting is the much-heralded trial day.

Once a month, the veterans steam up one of the restored locomotives. The 1925 Ansaldo shakes itself into motion, axles squealing and grating, finally leaving the depot in a cloud of steam. Two men perch on the steps to the cab, monitoring her behaviour. All the old-timers are gathered round, watching eagle-eyed for the slightest sign of trouble, oilcans in hand, ready to step in. One runs ahead to switch the locomotive to a different track, using the only set of points that is still operational. In any case, the Ansaldo will not go far; the war spared only two hundred yards of track at Asmara station.

It will take another two years to link the *ferrovia* to the Red Sea. The railway will be Eritrea's riposte to the colonial system; it is as if she is launching her own, single-handed campaign of conquest, enjoying the dignity won at such a cost. Provided, of course, the horrors of war do not return...

OPPOSITE: Typical of Eritrea's veterans, Seyoum Beraki, 75, is works foreman at Asmara station. All his energy is devoted to co-ordinating the efforts of veterans and volunteers.

1. and 2. Jean-Claude Guillebaud, *La Porte des larmes*, Seuil, 1996.

Afar, Tigre, Tigrinya; conscripts,
Ethiopian army deserters ...
More than 300 workers from every ethnic
group in this part of the Horn of Africa
are occupied in rebuilding the railway.

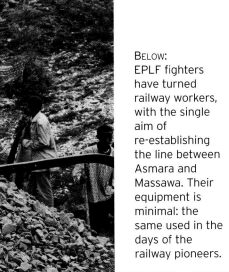

BELOW:
EPLF fighters have turned railway workers, with the single aim of re-establishing the line between Asmara and Massawa. Their equipment is minimal: the same used in the days of the railway pioneers.

OVERLEAF:
A primitive way of bending rails.

The people of Damas village have turned out to rebuild a bridge destroyed by torrential rain.

OVERLEAF: Work in progress at the foot of the Abyssinian plateau, near Damas.

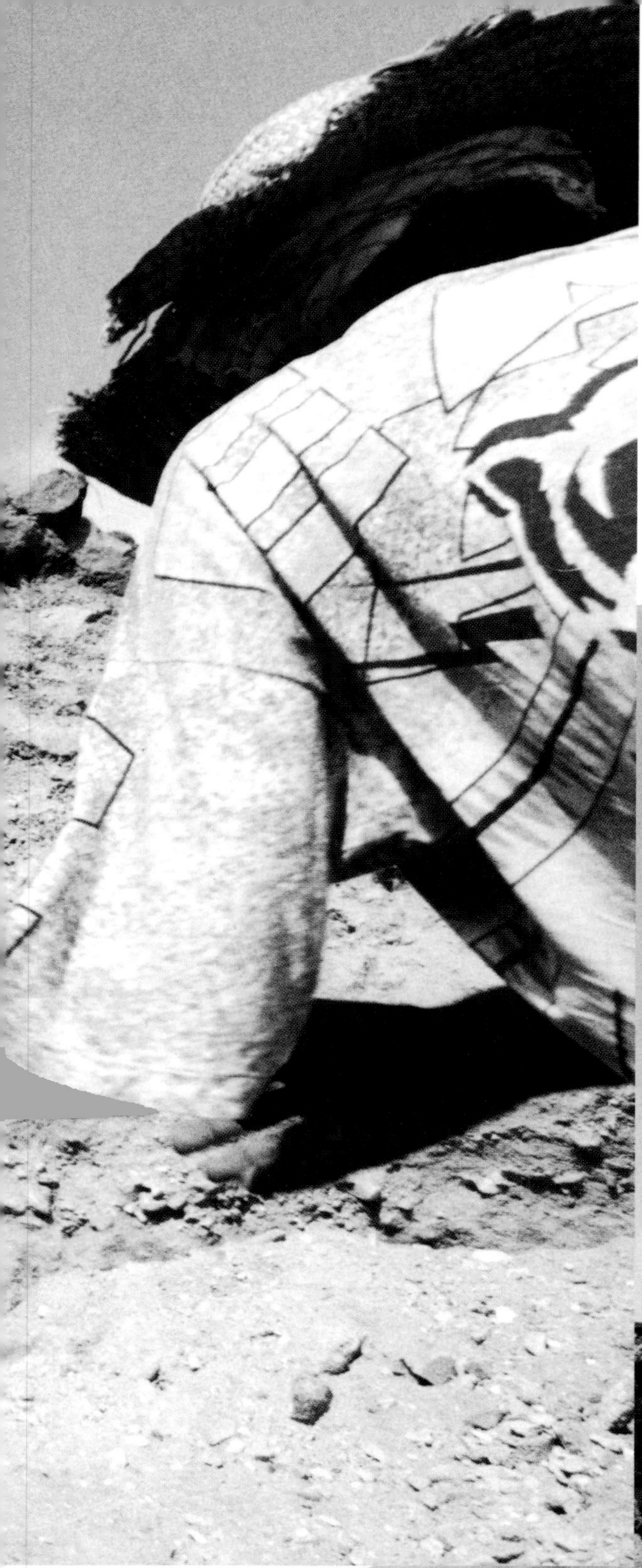

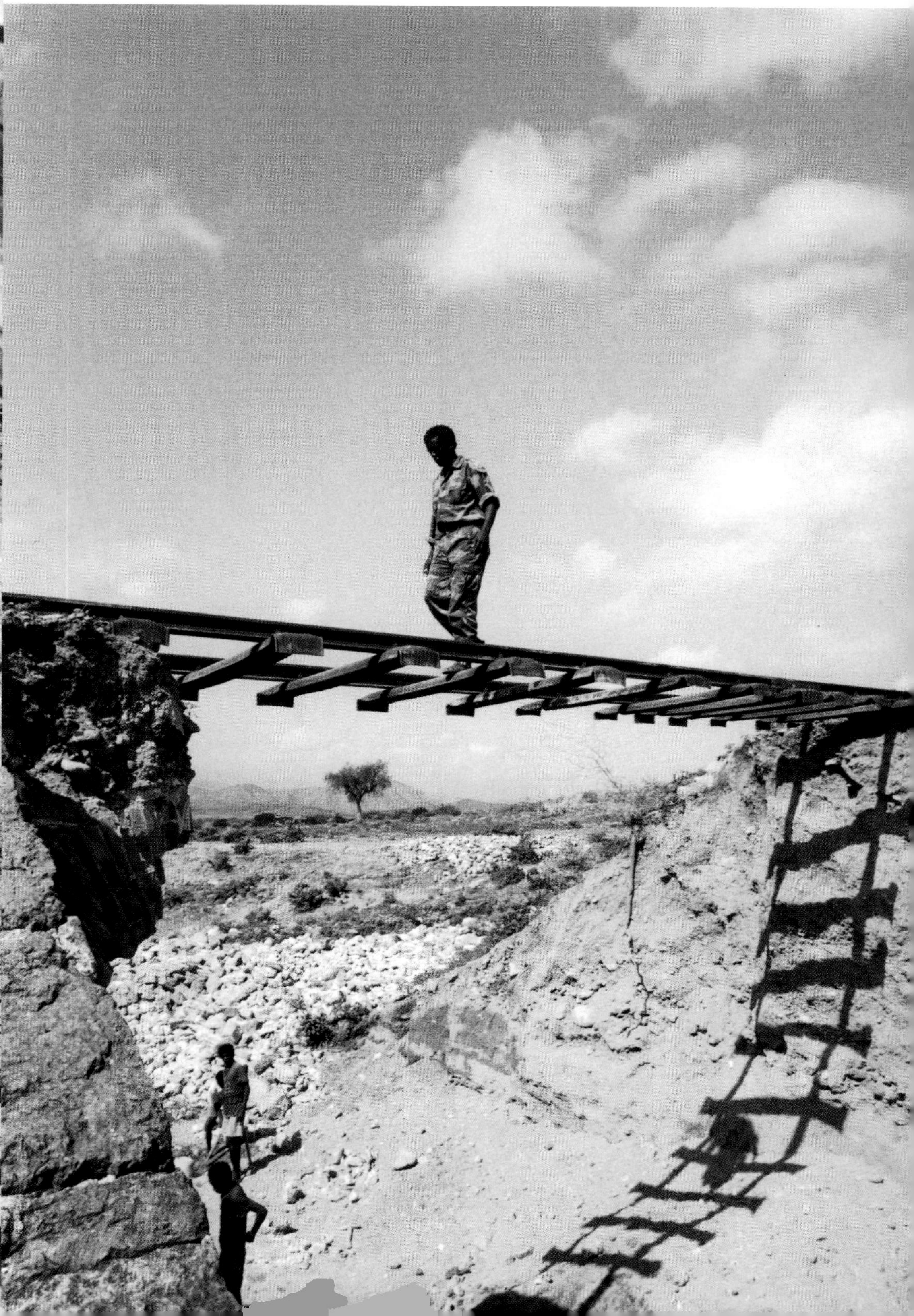

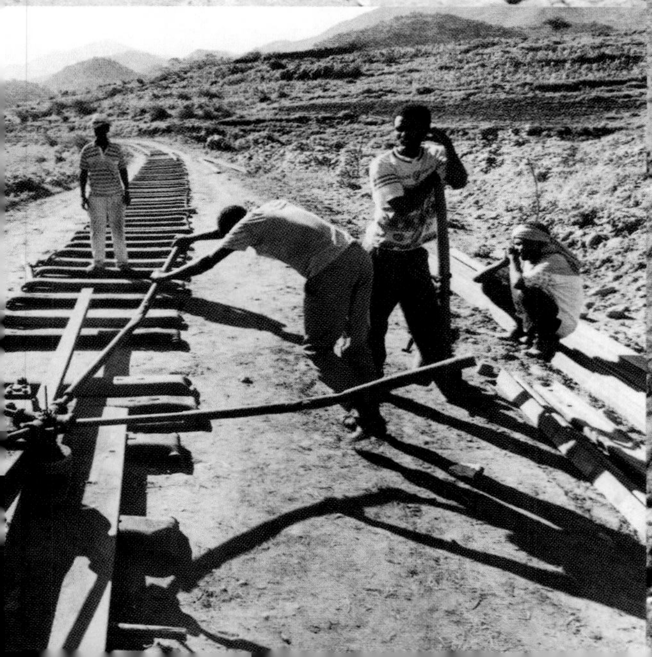

Along the dizzying escarpment which climbs
inexorably 73 miles (117 km) from the Red Sea
to the capital Asmara, there are no less than
30 tunnels and over 60 bridges and viaducts.

The reconstruction
work disrupts the
passage of
nomads:
shepherds and
camel drivers who
have used the
dismantled line for
over 20 years.

"In this Arab-African area of North Africa, the citadel of Abyssinia thrusts itself like a sheer promontory out above the Red Sea ..." J.-C. Guillebaud *La Porte des larmes*. These walls of rock presented the Italians with an incredible challenge when building the rail line. Today, the Eritreans intend to reconquer the route, whatever the cost.

"Little by little, the country's single rail line is being reconstructed like a Meccano model. What provided munitions for war will now serve the cause of peace. This line tells everything about the country: its poverty, and its determination."

Jean-Claude Guillebaud
La Porte des larmes

Osman, Idriss and Tagai were drivers or fitters between the 1930s and the 1950s. Twenty-five railway veterans, amazingly sprightly for their age, are resurrecting the technology that shaped their youth.

"My heart leaps whenever I see a train about to slip out along the polished rails which girdle and encircle the Earth."

Joseph Kessel *Wagon-lit*

Repaired
locomotives are
tested once a
month on the 200
yards of track
spared by the war
at Asmara station.
The old-timers
watch eagle-eyed
for any sign of a
problem. These
locomotives are
reawakening after
a 20-year sleep in
their sheds.

OVERLEAF:
A Russian Ural
truck, captured
from the
Ethiopians and
mounted on a
bogie, about to
test the track.

Last Train for Darjeeling

– the "Toy Train"

The world's second largest rail network is about to return its "Magnificent Titans" to the sheds for the last time. India has methodically been phasing out steam railways in recent years. Rail remains dominant as the nation's lifeline, but the sight of billowing white vapour and the shriek of whistles are virtually things of the past. Yet the symbolic Darjeeling Himalayan Railway (DHR), known as the "Toy Train", a unique form of mountain railway, is fighting a rearguard action on the steep slopes lush with tea plantations. Here, on these Himalayan foothills, steam will draw its last breath.

Darjeeling, "the ultimate desire, way up in the blue yonder". The name, which comes from the Tibetan *Dorge Ling* (meaning "City of Thunder"), is perfectly attuned to this city clinging to the mountain between earth and sky. Darjeeling is never sure where it belongs: above or below the clouds. One is constantly forced to adapt to its changing moods: all year long, the air and sky are in tumult. On the Himalayan foothills, between the flat, furnace-like plains of western Bengal and the eternal snows of the roof of the world, it is the clouds and mists that rule the weather. At a whim they swallow the zinc-roofed houses straggling down the crests, the tea plantations on the escarpments, and the monarch who controls Darjeeling's destiny – the legendary summit of Kanchenjunga.

There is nowhere like Darjeeling, perched at a modest 7,000 ft (2,134 m), for watching the mists swirling up in wave after wave from the valley floors like an advancing army, besieging the treetops. With a

PRECEDING PAGES: Chaos at Tindharia station.

OPPOSITE: "Carriages still faithful to the cumbersome beauty of the stagecoach." Paul Nizan, *Antoine Bloyé*. In a train "one is, as it were, leaning against a moving barrier, or sealed inside the torpedo of eternity as it pierces the armour of time." Jacques Réda *L'Herbe des talus*.

little patience, one can make out the whistling of a locomotive echoing up towards the line of the peaks. Everywhere else, the sound is joyful and bracing; here, it rises above the hamlets like a prolonged wail issuing from inside the mountain. Somewhere, under the frothing, writhing clouds, a train is labouring up the slopes, as it has done every day since 1881.

The DHR is probably the only railway in existence that shares right of way with a mountain road for its whole length. Here, tarmac takes second place to rail, and for a while longer steam locomotives will rule the road leading to the Himalayan sanctuary. Trains even usurp the main streets of the villages, where people hold their breath each time one comes spluttering and puffing through. The restrictions they impose on road traffic, already perilous enough in India, have given birth to a generation of madcap drivers – despite the warning signs littering the verges. However, the Indian authorities responsible for the highway code have not been lacking in imagination. Amongst the delightful pearls of wisdom are *Drive slow to enjoy the beauty of hill* (although this, taken literally, is liable to have fatal consequences for the driver, given the absolute necessity of keeping one's eyes on the road in these parts), *Keep your nerves on a sharp curve,* and *It is better to be fifteen minutes late in this world than fifteen minutes earlier in the next.*

The total length of the tortuous, narrow-gauge rail route is 60 miles (90 km), rising up in the process to a height of 7,407 ft (2,258 m) at Ghum before descending for the last short stretch into Darjeeling. The locomotives were manufactured by Sharp Stewart (Glasgow) between 1880 and 1925; they manage the climb more or less happily. It takes nine hours to make the chaotic ascent to Darjeeling – when there are no breakdowns or other unforeseen calamities. With such a timetable – not to mention its disastrous profitability – the Himalayan train provides ammunition for the radical road lobby, which is fighting (with the aid of large-scale corruption) for the line's closure. Fortunately, in November 1999, UNESCO included the line on its list of World Heritage Sites, encouraged no doubt by pressure from foreign steam enthusiasts. There are, for example, DHR railway societies in both England and Australia, whose members exchange information on the Internet, liaise with the Indian authorities and organise regular trips to Darjeeling.

The whole story began with a certain Dr Campbell, a representative of the British East India Company. In 1838, he sowed this mountainous desert with a few tea plants imported from China. Ten years later, Darjeeling boasted 10,000 inhabitants. Around 1860, in the days of the Raj, British government officials, exhausted by Calcutta's disease-ridden climate,

established their summer quarters at Darjeeling, which reminded them of the misty Scottish Highlands. Under their supervision, the tea plantations or "tea gardens" began to burgeon on the Himalayan slopes. The tea known as Darjeeling was born; the name is synonymous with quality, and uttered with reverence today. All that remained was the problem of transport. Problem soon solved: the locomotives from Glasgow would deal with that. The "Toy Train", as the British called it, was born.

In the mid-twentieth century, Darjeeling became the fashionable holiday resort for the Bengali middle classes of Calcutta. In 1962, the legendary film-maker Satyajit Ray immortalised this romantic Himalayan city in *Kanchenjunga*. The spectacular scenery and the acrobatic course of the railway helped establish Darjeeling as the starting point for grand adventures in the Himalayas. Thirty-odd engines used to maintain a permanent service, with up to twelve journeys a day. Now, despite the incessant strikes by truck drivers who supply the coal and the derailments caused by the parlous state of the track, the valiant surviving locomotives manage just one return trip daily.

The undisputed star of them all is 779B. Her 1892 vintage has earned her unanimous respect, even amongst the most fervent advocates of diesel. Every day, she sets off with the same flourish on her tortuous and peril-fraught journey. Things have not changed since the 1930s, when Henri Michaux reported in *Un Barbare en Asie* after his long journey through India, "She takes the curves like a bicycle; nothing upsets her. She advances, reverses, describes loops and spirals, twisting and turning back on herself."

In the enervating heat of New Jalpaiguri on the northern plains of Bengal, 779B is steamed up by dawn. Her livery is freshly repainted royal blue; the plate on her side bears her name in gold letters *Himalayan Bird*. Inside the suffocating cab, the fireman, undaunted, shovels coal into the firebox with precision and vigour.

The matrons in the first-class compartments implore the train to start, waving their fans through the windows and delicately plucking at the gaudy, shimmering saris draped round their shoulders. There is little difference between first and second class, except that the latter is more crowded and the seats here are less plush. But in first class, the women have those well-rounded bodies betraying their social origins. Caste notwithstanding, their flocks of lanky, insolent teenagers are clamouring for food and already the mamas are digging into copious supplies. At this season of the year, the middle classes of Calcutta and Delhi make a mass exit for the refreshing heights of Darjeeling.

Most of the locomotives are Baldwins manufactured in Scotland between 1880 and 1925. The earliest were climbing the Himalayas back in 1881.

The second-class passenger has only to fork out the derisory sum of 20 rupees to reach the Himalayan terminus. His toughest problem is keeping his place from being pinched if he wants to survive this epic nine-hour trip. This has already dawned on a Danish tourist, a larger-than-life character wearing a stunned expression; he is solidly riveted to his seat, pinioned between two hefty, crag-faced Nepalese.

Rattling happily along, we reach the last station on the plain, Siliguri Junction, interchange for Nepal, Bhutan and the ex-kingdom of Sikkim. After passing through the little red-and-white-fronted station at Skuna, the difficulties begin. A banking engine arrives and is coupled to the rear of the train; the gradients are steepest on the first third of the ascent. The centenarian locomotives enter battle, fireboxes belching flames, in the middle of a sumptuous forest of silk-cotton trees and royal poincianas which might well conceal a few surviving tigers. How can these tiny 0-4-0 locomotives expect to conquer the foothills of the Himalayas? Each of these roaring cauldrons requires a crew of five: the driver, hanging on to the whistle for dear life as soon as the rails begin to share right of way with the road; a coal-breaker, perched on the bunker smashing blocks of coal non-stop with a hammer; a fireman to shovel it into the firebox; and two sanders squatting towards the front of the boiler – they spread sand on the rails to slow the locomotive's descent and prevent the wheels sliding on the way up. There are also four brakemen operating the brakes in the carriages.

The forest thins out as we approach Tindharia, and we begin to glimpse the tea gardens. The small, compact bushes are soon evident, clothing the folds of the mountainside, looking for all the world like ribbons of dark green corduroy. In Tindharia station, picturesquely situated at the base of a vegetation-covered cliff, the *Queen of the Hills* (No. 804), just down from Darjeeling, idles, sighing jets of steam, waiting for the up train to pass before continuing her descent to the plain. Low cloud is already masking the outlines of the

foothills, and the passengers can enjoy their first breaths of cool air.

Close by, Tindharia's depot forms the DHR's base. In primitive conditions, virtuoso fitters perform miracles so that every day old ladies can travel up the mountain. But anyone wanting to penetrate this sanctum and take a few harmless photos will need to engage in a bureaucratic contest with the authorities. The Indians are almost paranoid about the security of their infrastructure; it is intriguing to imagine what sinister foreign presence might be interested in this decrepit old shed with its collection of Puffing Billies. Nonetheless, the employees at Tindharia proudly show visitors the monumental restoration work they have carried out on *Baby Shivok*, a little marvel born in 1881 in the German factories of Orenstein and Koppel.

For over half a century, the DHR transported the world's finest tea. Now, relays of trucks bring it down to the plain of Bengal three times more quickly.

Back to the slopes. The *Himalayan Bird* takes a tight bend, then returns almost to the start of the curve to tackle the crazy loop known as Agony Point, teetering over a sheer drop. It is like something out of a cartoon. At certain points, "Z reverses" are used to make the going easier: the train reverses up the oblique stroke of the Z, then sets off again on the new level.

In the half-deserted hamlets, the line passes close to the doorsteps of vividly painted houses. When we arrive in the larger community of Kurgeong ("City of the White Orchids" in Tibetan), the continuous screeching of the whistle mingles with the hooting of car horns. In the middle of a tiny square also serving as the station, a harassed policeman attempts to direct the train through a seething mass of vehicles. Chaos of every type reigns here; the scene's participants at this altitude are predominantly Bhutanese, Tibetans and Nepalese. Describing the DHR, Henri Michaux observed: "Everywhere there are smiles; small, delicate, unforced smiles. These smiles of the eastern races are the most beautiful in the world, I think." (*Un Barbare en Asie*).

In first class, the matrons decide to abandon ship. Fed up with the slow crawl and the discomfort, the soot infiltrating their hair and the cumulative effect of so many brushes with danger, they decide to proceed to Darjeeling by car.

The thundering procession of carriages restarts, winding down the main street, seeking an escape route through the maze of overflowing stalls that flirt with the rails, only 18 inches (50 cm) away, the locomotive shooting jets of steam over the displays of spices and vegetables.

Visitors from Calcutta flock to Darjeeling's heights, a temporary refuge from the suffocating heat of the Bengal summer.

This is the ritual hour when everything grinds to a halt in the little town of Kurgeong; with unfailing curiosity, the locals stand and gawp at the angry creature storming its way through their midst in a shower of soot and sparks.

Clouds shred into rags on the summits of the odd-looking pines now mantling the slopes. At kilometre 73, the train derails; the ground is waterlogged, and the spikes and clips cannot hold the track in place. Stationary and defenceless, 779B waits to be rescued by the "railway ambulance". The road parapet becomes a perch for a group of laid-back baboons who are quite unmoved by the railway activity. Seizing his opportunity, one tries to climb in a carriage window and steal a titbit. Uproar among the passengers. An hour later, two simple jacks suffice to manoeuvre the locomotive back onto the tracks. Child's play, really.

Rain is falling over Sonada. A scrawny Sherpa, back bent under a pyramid of bricks, sloshes barefoot in the black mud through which streak the gleaming rails. Trackside, huge white stupas drown in the mist. Then a muffled, monotonous wail descends the mountain: in full religious dress, a ghostly procession of lamas slowly emerges from the gloom, cymbals and giant horns overwhelming the train's racket. Their long, blackish-brown cocked hats flap about in the fog; a rainbow of banners waves against the sky in counterpoint. The rain intensifies. The monks of Sonada, celebrating the annual feast of the Lord Buddha (Purnima), take refuge under the station awning, while elegant Tibetan women offer them cereals.

The train resumes its feverish course. On the outskirts of the village it brushes past a string of banners displaying Buddhist texts. "The route passes between floating prayers attached to the trees. Then the Himalayas and their snowbound peaks burst into view." (Henri Michaux).

"Train journeys are a form of theatre rich in 'situations'; the stations places both of wonder and tragedy."

Marcel Proust

At Ghum station the petite biscuit-seller makes excellent tea at her stall. This is a favourite venue for conversation with Limbu, the conductor, while savouring a pure form of Darjeeling promoted by local merchants as "the champagne of teas". Limbu's curiosity prompts him to ask me whether English is also the official language of the French. Imagine his astonishment when he discovers that a big country like France was never part of the British Empire.

For the last few miles, schoolboys hitch free rides, clinging to the coaches. A ray of sunshine pierces the mist, greeting the *Himalayan Bird* as she sets about the last, aerial loop at Batasia. Beyond stands the phenomenal mass that is the "roof of the world", buried somewhere in the cloud-packed sky behind the city of Darjeeling. For a second or two, Kanchenjunga emerges from its hiding place, revealing its 28,209-ft (8,598-m) peak, as if, with this fleeting gesture, to salute 779B's arrival in Darjeeling station.

Fare-dodgers: boys habitually hitch a ride to school in Kurgeong by clinging to the carriages.

FOLLOWING PAGES: A train fights its way down Kurgeong's main street.

A crowd of stowaways leaps onto the packed train. "A train taking the gradient... howling and whistling, abandoning everything, disappearing, swallowed by the earth, a prolonged shudder causing the ground to tremble."

Émile Zola *La Bête humaine*

OPPOSITE PAGE, TOP, AND ABOVE: Most travellers on the DHR are Nepalese, Tibetans or Bhutanese. According to Henri Michaux: "The Nepalese have chosen to live in the world's highest country... Among them the Gurkhas - stocky and unflinching, you can see the bravery in their eyes - are the very opposite of the Hindus." (*Un Barbare en Asie*).

LEFT: Water halt in a misty pine forest. The crew have filled the locomotive's tanks from a stream.

ABOVE:
The 56-mile (90-km) ascent on narrow-gauge track is beset with countless technical problems.

LEFT:
Gasping for breath, the old Baldwin struggles daily to 7,875 ft (2,400 m). Mist and steam drift about her steel frame. "Her bronze flanks dripped with a scalding perspiration." Théophile Gautier *Un Tour en Belgique.*

"Along the looping tracks trains pass like whirlwinds. Or fiendish mechanical toys. Some trains never meet. Others get lost along the way." Blaise Cendrars *Du monde entier*. This is almost what happens here, on the Batasia loop, just before Darjeeling.

"It rains tea in Darjeeling."
Kenneth White *Les Limbes incandescents*. This crop is regarded as the "champagne of teas". Clinging to the slopes of the foothills 3,000–6,000 ft (1,000–2,000 m) up, the tea gardens provide three harvests a year.

At Sonada, a hamlet on the way to Darjeeling, Tibetan lamas celebrate the annual feast of the Lord Buddha. In full religious dress, their procession crosses the track before skirting the little station dating from 1883. OVERLEAF: Darjeeling train approaching Tindharia.

The Little Trains of Java

On the foothills of volcanoes, in villages isolated amid rice fields, on the outskirts of overcrowded cities, an army of little steam engines trundles back and forth across the island of Java. During the cane harvest, these hundred-year-old machines, dedicated to the sugar industry, work a labyrinth of narrow-gauge lines unique in the whole world.

The blinding midday light floods through the cabin windows of the Garuda Boeing 727. It is the height of the dry season; on the approach to Java, with its 121 volcanoes, the sun looks as if it has fallen from the sky into an immense green plantation. Java – "mortal, divine, teeming with life"[1] – sprawls between the Indian Ocean and the Java Sea, not far from the Equator, in a region where the heat is unrelenting throughout the year. A tangle of irrigated fields and teeming suburbs precedes the runway of Solo (Surakarta) submerged under the shimmering heat haze. This gateway to Indonesia, in the heart of the island and with its enticing, provincial atmosphere, seems a thousand times preferable to Jakarta, the country's capital, where everything is on a giant scale.

Two hours' drive from Solo, the museum-station of Ambarawa houses fifty-odd locomotives, former monarchs of the rails, now slumbering for ever on their pedestals. This is the inevitable starting point in any quest for the last traces of Java's steam trains. The majority of locomotives at Ambarawa originated in Germany between 1890 and 1920 and remained functional until 1986, a black year which saw steam disappear from main lines in Indonesia. They are still in a remarkable state of preservation.

RIGHT:
Activity is
always intense
in the depot
workshops at
Pajarakan,
eastern Java.

The Ambarawa line is the last passenger route, serving two small, antiquated stations – Bedono and Jambu – along a bare 5.5 miles (9 km) of track. Last relic it may be, yet it captures in a nutshell the golden age of Indonesian rail travel, weaving among the little rice fields before ascending a hill thick with banana trees and giant bamboos. The train crosses a grey and rusted steel bridge, scarcely visible amongst the luxuriant vegetation. On either side of the bridge lie chessboards of tiny paddies, their perimeters planted with banana and coconut trees, and reached along narrow, elevated causeways. Now and again, these paths are blocked by plots of tomato seedlings displaced from the fields by lack of space. During a trip to Java in the 1950s, Roger Vailland noted: "Between the foothills, I spotted rice plantations no bigger than the size of a dinner table back home in Beauce."[2] The locomotive passes. When quiet returns, the only sounds are the croaking of frogs in the paddies that mirror the sky, the cries of children driving off marauding birds with catapults, and the rustling of the wind in the huge branches of the banana trees.

During the cane harvest from June to September, more than a hundred engines, some centenarians, resume intense activity after their annual hibernation, meandering indefatigably between plantations and mills along narrow-gauge tracks laid in the 1920s. The most common gauge here is 2 ft 3 $^9/_{16}$ in (700 mm), as opposed to the Indonesian standard gauge of 3 ft 6 in (1.067 m). The Frenchman, Paul Decauville (1846–1922), was the pioneer of the system of lightweight locomotives and narrow-gauge railways used to transport sugar cane around Java since the start of the twentieth century.

In the 1930s, there were more than 50 sugar mills on the island. The Dutch, the then colonial power, did not boast a rail industry, and were forced to import essential machinery from their German neighbours. Most of these engines are from the Orenstein & Koppel stable; their liveries vary from company to company. The turbulent course of Java's twentieth-century history explains in part the locomotives' extraordinary longevity. First came the Japanese invasion, then the civil war, and finally independence; the result was that the sugar industry remained trapped in time for around 30 years.

At 6.30 am, the streets of Solo resemble an ants' nest as they swarm with cycle rickshaws. A vast throng of workers – poor, but proud and resigned to their fate – comes to life in the silvery white dawn. The light of the rising sun is already diffracted and scattered by the city's pollution. Enclaves of rice plantations survive amid the urban chaos. The traveller will wait in vain for city and countryside to suddenly part company; the suburbs go on for ever, swallowing

> "Give me the light, easy breathing
> Of tall, slender locomotives that move so gracefully."
>
> Valéry Larbaud *Barnabooth*

ABOVE:
A 1921 Orenstein & Koppel idling in the cane fields provides railwaymen with shade for an impromptu card game.

the villages that border the potholed ribbons of roads. Finally, one glimpses the cane plantations scattered in small lots round Ceper Baru mill.

A maze of rails fringes the factory, crosses the road and finally divides into individual lines heading out along the narrow embankments of the paddies to the distant cane fields. The locomotive depot is part of the plant, as at the other 57 mills in Java. Between the tracks, the ballast is littered with bagasse, the residue of cane stalks after extraction of the juice, a more or less permanent deposit that continues well out beyond the railway into the fields. These cultivated areas are modest in size and more like small gardens, so intense and uniform is their green.

Just around a clump of giant bamboos, is what looks like a slumbering steel beast, motionless on a curve of track. This locomotive exhales regular sighs, hushed but peaceful, as if nothing could disturb her. She rests there snoring in the middle of the paddies, solitary, with no one in the cab, as if she had always been part of the landscape. She is a 1912 Orenstein & Koppel, waiting on one of the precarious banked inclines for a train. In the distance, behind the absurdly tall plantations, a pair of white water buffaloes are hauling up three wagons loaded with cane. Each one contains up to six tons. The animals follow the line of the track, the driver cracking his whip as they struggle to keep their balance. Like in some ancient ritual, a string of 15 wagons is formed up, using buffalo power. The locomotive emerges from her torpid slumber; spitting embers, she is linked to the train and a stupendous clashing and

clanking of buffers and couplings signals the start of an epic haul to the mill gates. There, bare-chested men are heaving sugar bales into wagons marshalled by reluctant white buffaloes. For a few rupees a day, the underprivileged sugar workers load and unload the endless convoys shunting round the smoky complex. A remarkable number of security guards stroll about the perimeter, hiding their lack of concern behind dark glasses.

The locomotive comes to a halt beneath the immense canopy of frangipani trees that shelters the wagon yard; there the porters begin work on the new trucks, backs bent beneath weights of 220 lb (100 kg). One of the workers delves into a jute sack and offers me a handful of brown sugar. A cloud of whitish chaff flies out of the locomotive's cab. This is bagasse, processed at the mill into large cubes and used to fuel 90 per cent of the locomotives. Very light, bulky and volatile, it burns very quickly; the railway workers wear masks to protect their lungs from the dust. The locomotive tenders being too small, the pile of bagasse necessarily spills over into the cab, with only the fireman's head emerging from the mound. Struggling in the middle of this heap, he stuffs fuel in great armfuls into the locomotive's belly. The train sets off, whistle yelping. The crossing keeper half opens an eye and waggles his toe to operate the cord controlling the barrier. Leaving the "labyrinth of the wagon yard"[3], the engine seems to stagger, and this movement is transmitted all along the wagons, scattering a shower of rebellious cane stalks here and there.

On the foothills of Mt Lawu, a mist-shrouded volcano, two women selling cloves call out to some railwaymen at the entrance to Goranggareng village. Further on, young schoolgirls in uniform, with their ochre veils, are walking along the bagasse-strewn track. Goranggareng was robbed of its tranquillity a long while ago. The life of the village operates to the rhythm of the daily trains, as the railway shares the main road linking the factory to the loading point. The whole place is immersed in the spicy, intoxicating odour of sugar cane; one's skin feels sticky with particles swept up by the wind.

The streets echo to the tumultuous contest between cycle rickshaws and steam locomotives. Everything "moves to this rhythm; it is the pulse of life, the passing of time marked by the ticking of a clock".

Jacques Réda *L'Herbe des talus*

It is now 5pm, and the sun sinks with little warning. The track passes through one of the poor quarters, crosses a river on a metal bridge, then skirts more houses, zigzagging along narrow streets heavy with the scent of cloves, before disappearing beneath a magnificent vault of bamboo, whose towering tops creak in the breeze. Emerging from amongst these monumental grasses, it plunges into a maze of cane fields. The light tips of the plants undulate gently and the horizon above them is filled with black clouds. Suddenly one senses the puffing of a locomotive, an intermittent murmur in the distance. The mass of vegetation deadens all echoes; all that is audible is a gentle, easy breathing, in time with the muffled panting of the cylinders.

A superb Luttermöller appears between two stands of cane. She is the queen of Java's locomotives, with her three independent bogies: a great technical refinement making her incomparably easy to handle, especially on the curves.

Soon the place is deserted; the Luttermöller's crew seem to have abandoned her. The sun disappears behind the plantations where now there reigns unchallenged "that profound but vibrant silence of a locomotive at rest, full of little cries, sudden creakings, and sighings in the tangle of tubes."[4]

OPPOSITE PAGE: An enormous canopy of frangipani trees protects the wagon yard of this mill, which functions day and night during the sugar harvest.

LEFT: A locomotive smokestack dominates the lonely plantations.

1. Jules Michelet *La Montagne*
2. Roger Vailland *Borobodour*
3. Jacques Réda *La Tourne*
4. ibid.

ABOVE: Feeding the boiler with bagasse - the discarded cane stalks.
BELOW: Locomotives often stand idle for hours in the plantations, attracting curious children.

ABOVE: Cleaning the smokebox. Workers wear masks to protect their lungs from the cane dust.
BELOW: For want of a better place, a peasant dries his tobacco crop beside the track.

"... the iron horse is a living creature. You can hear it breathing as it rests, grumble when it starts, neigh as it runs; it sweats, trembles, pants, whinnies, slows to a trot, breaks into a gallop. All along its route it scatters its waste of burning coals and jets of boiling steam ..."

Victor Hugo (in a letter to his wife Adèle)

PRECEDING PAGES:
On duty
supervising
locomotive
movements at
the Pakis Baru
depot.

ABOVE AND LEFT:
Unlike in Cuba,
women work
the fields in
Java. They wear
several layers of
clothing as
protection
against the
pitiless sun and
injuries from the
tall, sharp cane
stalks.

Along field boundaries, buffaloes drag wagons overflowing with cane to be added to the apparently interminable trains for the mills. In isolated areas, the cane is brought to the railway on road trucks.

"German locomotives lack the nervous power of those made in Britain or Belgium..." Gérard de Nerval *Loreleï*.

A train emerges, rocking from side to side, from the labyrinth of a huge plantation, only for a wagon to derail a few hundred yards down the line. Here, in eastern Java, near the village of Asembagus, a few men and a good lever suffice to get things moving again.

FOLLOWING PAGES: The Ambarawa-Jambu line, last vestige of the old Indonesian network, runs through miles of banana groves and rice fields.

In Search of the

African Dream

From the southernmost tip of Africa to the meandering Zambezi, trains recapturing the romance of steam's golden age are embarking on a new era of railway conquest. Cape Town, the Garden Route, Pretoria, Bulawayo, the Victoria Falls: a great railway adventure haunted by the unfulfilled dream of Cecil Rhodes – to link the Cape with Cairo.

PRECEDING PAGES: The mining district of Wankie, just before the Victoria Falls.

OPPOSITE: David Livingstone, a Scottish physician, discovered the "Land of the Thundering Water". Constructed over the second gorge, the steel Falls Bridge separates Zimbabwe from Zambia. The bridge was built as close to the raging torrent as possible because Cecil Rhodes said he wanted travellers to hear the roaring of the Falls and feel the spray on their faces.

During the reign of Queen Victoria, when "the sun never set on the British Empire", an adventurer with unbounded imagination dreamed of connecting the Crown's African colonies at both extremes of the continent. In this time of insatiable desire for conquest, Cecil John Rhodes, the prime minister of Cape Colony and founder of the De Beers diamond mining company, launched an audacious project to construct a rail line from Cape Town to Cairo. A legendary figure whose visionary gifts were focused more on the economic expansion than the political future of southern Africa, Rhodes was in the habit of declaring: "The railway is my right hand, the telegraph my voice." Under his dynamic influence the work began.

Starting from Cape Town, the line crossed the frontier of Transvaal to Johannesburg, then in the grip of gold fever. From Johannesburg, it headed off to Pretoria – capital of the former Boer Republic – and on to Bulawayo over the featureless wastes of the bush. From there it traversed what was to become Rhodesia, later Zimbabwe, before spanning the Victoria Falls. In 1905, the dream of the world's most famous diamond magnate seemed to be on its way to becoming reality when the first train crossed the gorge. But Rhodes had died three years

earlier and so never saw the Falls Bridge. The components of this amazing feat of engineering were manufactured in Darlington, England; binding the two banks of this raging cauldron like a massive steel corset, it marked the first victory in the railway's conquest of Africa.

But the Empire broke up before the extremities of the continent could be linked and, a century later, the dream of a line running from the north to the south of the continent still remains unrealised. Nonetheless, some incredible routes are still to be enjoyed in southern Africa. Pretoria, now more acceptable to the international community since the demise of apartheid, has taken on the challenge of resurrecting some of the great trains from the glory days of steam.

Knysna. A heavy, coppery cloud hangs over the station, threatening to deluge the passengers crowded along the platform edge. The two locomotives that will pull the train along the Outeniqualand Preserved Railway to George (on the main Port Elizabeth-Cape Town route) are still being moved between the sheds and the little station with its grey slate roofs. A last squall from the Indian Ocean whips away the brilliant white steam of the two 1937-vintage Series 19 Ds. With a final clanking and clanging, the "Outeniqua-Choo-Tjoe" chuffs off along this branch of the Garden Route. But what does "Outeniqua" mean? The stationmaster mumbles that it might come from the Xhosa language: "Man laden with honey". No more precise information is proffered about this curiosity.

The traveller drifts away on the "tide of the railway". Reverie, intimate conversations ... or "time squandered on luxury".

Georges Marion "Le Rêve de Cecil Rhodes" (newspaper article)

Beyond all doubt, the 42-mile (67-km) route between Knysna and George is the most spectacular of the entire southern African littoral. One moment it is climbing through forests of pines and tree ferns, the next, spanning a succession of lagoons thronged with pink flamingos. It nibbles its way amongst mountains poised between earth and sky, soars over terrifying viaducts that stand like phantoms of stone imprisoned by the mists, strides across inlets where the sea roars and foams ... Knysna and George are unashamedly seaside resorts, but the journey between them is a thrill-seeker's paradise.

From George, the Union Limited takes over the section to Cape Town, using more powerful locomotives – but still steam. The route elbows its way between the Montagu mountains before twisting among foothills first planted with vines by the French Huguenots. The vast vineyards of Stellenbosch extend up to the gates of the destination city, Cape Town, whose exceptional site invests it with unique beauty. Symbol of the Rainbow Nation, squeezed

between Table Mountain and the Atlantic, the capital is desperate to lead this mosaic of a country towards a new and better future.

Cape Town. Philemon is an old white train driver from Maritzburg, in charge of the 800-ton Rovos service for Pretoria and the Falls, a seven-day journey. He chatters about the early days of the Trans-Karoo and the legendary trains on the route between the Cape and the Transvaal, which conveyed hordes of gold and diamond prospectors, troops mobilised for the Boer War, or carpetbaggers and immigrants in search of the "promised land". South Africa has persisted with steam power, owing to the abundance of coal in the region. Today, a score or more locomotives can be seen in steam.

Passing through the gates onto the platform at Cape Town, a series of pillars is revealed, plunged in a sinister twilight. Nothing reassuring or uplifting for the first-time traveller. But wait – elegant silhouettes are flitting towards the red carpet that leads to the boarding area. Rohan Vos, the train's owner, welcomes each with a glass of champagne. Since 1989, this visionary businessman has devoted his time and fortune to resurrecting the trains of the grand imperial days. Or, more prosaically perhaps, to achieving the ambitions of Cecil Rhodes. Vos, a descendant of the Batavian community, has restored the legendary Cape-Victoria Falls-Dar es Salaam route: 3,790 miles (6,100 km), 13 days' journey. The incomparably opulent and comfortable carriages are meticulous Edwardian restorations. To attract that very special class of passenger, this dream train has leaned heavily on nostalgia and refinement. Everything is designed to create an ambience of slow and stately travel – average

LEFT:
A Rovos dining car completely restored in Edwardian style. The luxury train with its impressive facilities makes the journey from Cape Town to Dar es Salaam in 13 days.

speed 28 mph (45 kph) – right down to the special suspension system, designed to dampen the slightest jolt. The Rovos train is not for going places but for wallowing in sheer luxury. Relaxation, reverie, intimate conversation is the name of the game – a far cry from the stress and compulsive haste of most modern travel.

Sober and undemonstrative, the train's departure arouses no particular emotions. No white handkerchiefs waved from the windows, no couple whispering strained farewells, putting off the moment in a risky last embrace, no portly stationmaster blowing strident blasts on his whistle. The veneered, openwork shutters are all closed, and the train seems to slink furtively out of the station. In the vast straggling suburbs, the line bisects the poor townships, and gloomy looks follow the progress of the elite Rovos and its slowly moving bottle-green cars labelled "Pride of Africa". A strange sensation. Only a few years ago, this train could never have

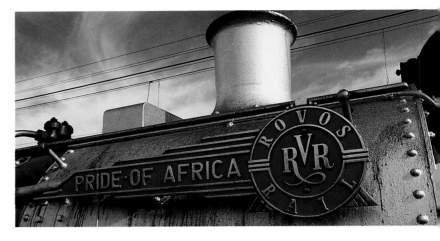

The "Pride of Africa": name board on a Series 19.

left the city. The names of the stations en route recall how many countries of Europe had colonies here: De Doorns, Wellington, Bellville... Then the lush valleys and misty mountains of the Cape give way to the vast wastes of the Great Karoo.

Each cabin bears the name of a southern African town, and to help passengers orientate themselves and strike up acquaintances, the names of the occupants are also inscribed. Examining the names, it seems that Mr Armstrong and Ms Adler are the only "illicit" couple aboard. They can hardly lose sight of one another amongst their 60-odd fellow passengers, as everywhere they go they carry their binoculars with them. In the evening, an Englishman, Charles – in suit and tie, the only permissible alternative to evening dress – relaxes in the dining car with its 1930s decor. He could just as easily be sitting in his London club, and he will soon be back there, telling everyone: "Despite all the Trans-whatevers I've travelled on in China and Russia and Europe, nothing can beat the Rovos for luxury..." Annie, an American for whom an excess of the Cape's Chardonnay holds no terrors, is writing postcards to her dogs' home in Connecticut. She has climbed up Machu Picchu and the steps of the Potala palace, but, she swears, from now on she is going nowhere if not by train.

As the Rovos glides into Pretoria, her locomotive releases alternate blasts of steam and black smoke. Haughtily indifferent, she draws to a halt in the elegant station, specially built for her by her owner. Already, porters in impeccable uniforms are bustling about the platform. The reconstruction is perfect; all that is missing is the period costume. A little way off, three gleaming locomotives (Series 19 Ds) await their next trains. Each sports the name of one of Rohan Vos's children: Shaun, Brenda, Bianca.

Forty-eight hours more are required to reach the Victoria Falls. This may seem a long time, but not if one wants to glimpse the quaint fishermen of the Hex River Valley, experience the suffocating heat of the Karoo Desert at sundown, enjoy the amazing mechanical ballet of steam locomotives shunting in Bulawayo station, or simply watch the antelopes and herds of elephants in Hwange National Park. Just south of Bulawayo, in Matopo National Park, Cecil Rhodes lies buried under a striking circle of weathered granite, a spot where he loved to sit and meditate.

Before reaching the Victoria Falls, the landscape becomes remarkably monotonous; during the southern winter, the bush turns every shade between ochre and grey as far as the eye can see. It is impossible to imagine a prettier station than "Vic' Falls", as it is customarily

abbreviated. Travellers weighed down with luggage wait serenely on the platform with its scattering of dwarf palms and bougainvillea. A few steps away is the hotel of the same name, recalling the sumptuous European establishments of a century ago. The station and the hotel are lavishly appointed, just as in the early years of the twentieth century, when they accommodated visitors from London. The final surprise is by no means the least: the view from the hotel terrace. There, suspended over the second gorge of the Zambezi, is the railway bridge, the amazing vestige of Cecil Rhodes's vision of joining Cape Town and Cairo. He had it built as near the water as possible, because, he said, he wanted train passengers to hear the roaring of the Falls and feel the spray on their faces.

Near the parapet high above the mist-filled gorge, a tall, slim male figure – inevitably British – calls out to two elegant females. "Oh, by the way, my name is Henry." Comes the distant echo: "Dr Livingstone, I presume?" Livingstone – the town, that is – is some six miles (10 km) from the Victoria Falls, across the river in Zambia. But that, one might say, is another Africa.

TOP:
The Safari Express Tea Train, with dining car staff in colonial uniforms (Victoria Falls Station).

LEFT AND ABOVE:
American-type "crossbuck" typical of the South African network.

TOP RIGHT:
Fireman at work,
Bulawayo station.
"In the red hot
pipes of the
massive boiler!"
Jules Verne *Paris
au XXe siècle*.

BELOW AND
OPPOSITE PAGE:
The gleaming
locomotives of
Rovos Rail (Series
19s) are the best
maintained in
South Africa.
"The overheated
monster fears no
rivals! Inside its
quivering shell it
roars and
bellows..." Jules
Verne *Paris au
XXe siècle*

"The railway is my right hand, the telegraph my voice," declared Cecil Rhodes. In 1905, the first train crossed the Victoria Falls.

LEFT:
Series 14, Victoria
Falls station.

BELOW, LEFT:
Rovos passengers
arriving at the
elegant little
Victoria Falls
station.

BELOW, RIGHT:
Livingstone
station,
immediately
after the Falls,
in Zambia.

ABOVE: A 1950s Series 20 scurries through the bush. BELOW: Bulawayo, Zimbabwe's second city, is the centre of operations for a score of remaining steam trains. OPPOSITE PAGE: Series 19 watering at Victoria Falls.

BULAWAYO

From the mists of the Indian Ocean between Port Elizabeth and Cape Town to the Victoria Falls, trains tirelessly strive to bring Cecil Rhodes's dream to life. On the 42-mile (67-km) branch line from Knysna to George, the Outeniqua follows part of the breathtaking Garden Route.

OVERLEAF: Heading towards Cape Town, among the humid forests bordering Knysna lagoon: part of the Garden Route.

The Last Bastion

of Steam in Europe

Not far from the German border, southwest of Poznan, the little town of Wolsztyn is the scene of a last stand. Its steam locomotive depot continues to function in the same way as it has for the last 85 years: a living museum in the heart of Wielkopolska.

There is an unreal air about nights at Wolsztyn station. A 1920s clock casts an eerie glow on the step of Witold's office; the motionless figure of the stationmaster is silhouetted against clouds of steam shimmering white in the darkness as he waits for the whistle of one of his snorting monsters. Looming massively, their dim forms seem to be sleeping all around the turntable. Rumblings and metallic tapping noises issue from the chaos of confused shadows. Under the old-style floodlights, great eddies of pale vapour sweep up and vanish in the black void. Three locomotives are steamed up, ready to leave the roundhouse, which accommodates ten engines and is classed as a historic monument. It dates from 1907 – like the watering and coaling systems, the turntable, the signalling, and the points (switches).

Wolsztyn, a small town of 10,000 souls, has proved remarkably faithful to its railway traditions. Between 1895 and 1906, the KPEV – Royal Prussian State Railways – transformed this peaceful lakeside community into a railway depot, which was to become one of Poland's most important when the country regained independence after the First World War. Today, a large staff maintains a collection of active steam locomotives, most of which are unique. This is one of the last railway depots left in Europe that regularly services locomotives for passenger trains.

Jerzy, who drives *La Belle Hélène*, has opened the cylinder cocks and sounded his whistle. A jet of steam emerges and quickly fades into the night. *La Belle Hélène* (PM 36–2) is a survivor of the series of prestige Polish steam locomotives manufactured before the Second World War. The board on her boiler housing, displaying the arms of Wolsztyn and the Polish white eagle, catches the light and gives off a golden glow in the darkness. The star of the depot inches onto the turntable. Now she is moving down the line, quivering a little as she crosses the other tracks, her powerful breast sweeping aside the shadows, until her huge wheels come to rest at

Jerzy checks the controls and prepares for the off. The sound of metallic shudders rings through the silent darkness. For the driver, love of the job never diminishes.

the platform. A final shudder as the carriages are coupled, while steam escaping from the heating system spreads all around. Waiting passengers dive inside to escape the bitter night. At the far end of the platform, Witold signals to the driver by swinging his lantern. An instant's silence. Steam hisses under the engine, the cylinders take up their musical beat. We're off to Poznan.

Several times a day, Wolsztyn's steam locomotives cover the 50 miles (80 km) separating this small town from the regional capital. This is a form of rail travel quite unique in Europe in the age of the high-speed train, a journey back in time punctuated all the way by halts at smart little brick-built stations. Among the most astonishing are those in the remote villages of Rostarewo and Rakoniewice. Everywhere we find a railway official adjusting his impeccable uniform and only too pleased to supply information. On its way to the heart of the ancient city of Poznan, the line passes through the Wielkopolska National Park with its famous pine and oak forests.

Howard Jones, who moved from Britain to Wolsztyn when he retired a few years ago, is fighting to keep the steam locomotives running. He has a passion that could only be British, and at first, he alarmed the authorities. But little by little, he made them realise the incredible heritage in their possession. Now, through *The Wolsztyn Experience*, a mutual trust railway society run in conjunction with PKP (Polish State Railways), he has developed a highly innovative method of funding locomotive maintenance: for a fee of several hundred pounds, steam buffs can learn to drive one. In Howard's cellar, transformed into a bar crammed with railway memorabilia, Alan Macfarlane, a British tourist, raises his glass of vodka with Wolsztyn's railway staff. Tomorrow, he will be let loose at the controls of *La Belle Hélène* and allowed to drive a passenger train all the way to Poznan. "There's no denying it," sighs Howard, "we're just overgrown kids!"

ABOVE: Trailing a turbulent white exhaust, a passenger train powers through the Wielkopolska forests en route to Poznan. BELOW: Down the line, "she bellows amid the confusion of trees and steam". Jacques Réda *La Tourne*.

LEFT AND BELOW
LEFT:
Day and night,
locomotives are
fired up. Several
passenger and
freight
departures a
day mean
round-the-clock
activity.

OPPOSITE PAGE:
"His whole
attention was
riveted on the
track and the
signals ahead...
He loved his
engine so much,
like an
accommodating
mistress, from
whom he
expected nothing
but happiness."
Émile Zola La
Bête humaine.

"Into chasms in the sky
Raging locomotives fly."

Blaise Cendrars *Du monde entier*

BELOW, LEFT:
Fifteen charming
little stations
punctuate the 50
miles (80 km)
between Wolsztyn
and Poznan.

BELOW, RIGHT:
Plumes of steam
swirl under the
depot floodlights.

OVERLEAF:
"This night is like
a hundred
thousand others
when a train is
hurtling through
the darkness."
Blaise Cendrars
Du monde entier.

The Loggers' Train:

The Mocanitza

In the north of the Eastern Carpathians, the Maramures Forest harbours an amazing railway beast: the Mocanitza. Every day since 1933, an ancient locomotive has been conveying loggers and timber wagons along the 30-mile (50-km) course of the Vaser valley. This train is the workers' only transport link with the outside world; it is also virtually the last steam train in Europe serving a commercial forestry operation.

PRECEDING PAGES: In a rickety, patched-up wooden wagon, loggers await the departure of the old train for the Vaser valley.

OPPOSITE PAGE: Locomotive graveyard at the railhead of Viseu de Sus. "So many happy memories cast away among the rust and brambles... And what have they done with the old locomotive?" Jacques Réda La Tourne.

The Romanians are incorrigible poets. Notebook in the pocket of his fur-lined coat, Gavril Ciuban plans an expedition into the forest in search of a pack of wolves which, say the loggers, has just crossed the frontier from Ukraine. His undemanding work at the Community Arts Centre of Viseu de Sus allows him unlimited scope for his hobbies: poetry and hunting. Erring understandably on the side of caution, Gavril is accompanied by a hard-faced hunter in a fetching green felt hat; his old Czech rifle is slung over his shoulder and cartridge pouches bulge at his waist. Lucian, a former forestry agent, has a feudal attitude: his only reason for existence is the forest, which he treats as his own domain. The two men wander along amongst the labyrinth of tracks lying buried under layers of snow and grease. They are waiting for the loggers' train, which, in theory, should have set out two hours ago.

On the edge of the small town of Viseu de Sus, the forestry railhead and the dilapidated warehouses surrounding it belong to Viseuforest SA. The company is quite happy to convey the occasional visitor, as there are no roads leading out of the Vaser valley. To protect themselves from

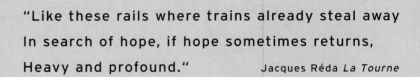

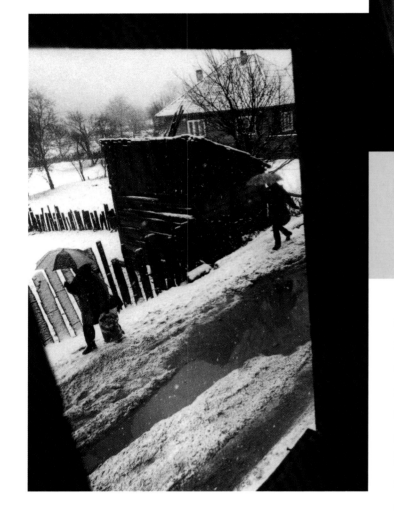

"Like these rails where trains already steal away
In search of hope, if hope sometimes returns,
Heavy and profound."
Jacques Réda *La Tourne*

the cold, some of the passengers have taken refuge in the forge. There, the railway staff eye them with a kind of amused superiority: without their skill in making a spare part for it, the train will not start. Mircea, in an Astrakhan hat, is the stationmaster: jovial but with something of a fixation – he is the only man in a hurry in the entire region of Maramures, determined to get this "swine of a train" started at any cost. His rapid strides take him up the narrow-gauge track – "0.76 m [2 ft 6 in]," he informs us – past a locomotive graveyard looking distinctly pathetic under its thick pall of snow, to the front of the train. Some very strong language – Mircea has looked in the cab and found the driver dead drunk.

The locomotive does not seem to be in a much better state. Wheezy, spewing jets of steam like an oversized kettle on wheels, she hardly looks fit for the seven-hour journey up the line. "A replica of a Hungarian 0-8-0T, 1955," Mircea shouts. "From the Resita Works, the oldest makers in Romania." Our mercurial stationmaster then decides to take things into his own hands. With a shove from his shoulder, he sends the poor dazed driver staggering among the coal, seizes the controls, opens the cylinder cocks and extracts a hysterical shriek from the whistle. The pointsman (switchman) is encouraged to "wake his ideas up". A volley of curses and Mircea decides to forget the missing part. He invites the passengers to embark: "Get yourselves inside, then!"

The locomotive, this grotesque black beast, may look all in, but she isn't finished yet. The fireman drags her back to life, pouring coal into the firebox; soon she is roaring away in her

quivering shell. Elated at seeing the machine regain her throbbing vitality, Mircea informs us that she will devour three tons of coal during her seven-hour trip. He has been working for the company (largely privatised a few years back) for 25 years. In the 1950s, there were some 3,725 miles (6,000 km) of forest track spanning the whole country. Today, only these 30 miles (50 km) remain, worked tirelessly by the same steam train. A hundred and thirty-four loggers manage around 75,000 acres (30,000 ha) out of a total forest area of 642,000 acres (260,000 ha); for them, the Mocanitza is a lifeline to the outside world.

The train shatters the silence of the last, sleepy hamlets before tackling the interminable ascent of the Vaser valley. On the face of this girl staring from the passenger car, resignation blends with an indefinable melancholy.

The Vaser valley threads through the Maramures mountains at an altitude of 2,300–5,000 ft (700–1,500 m). The last village before the line begins to ascend is Novat; its church thrusts a seemingly endless spire skywards, while heavy flakes of snow descend on sloping roofs made of oak tiles. Here, time is suspended in the limbo of a distant past. Again and again, the Mocanitza stops to pick up loggers who materialise all along the route. In the solitary passenger car, an old woman warms herself at a wood stove anchored to the rickety floor. Beside her in the shadows a forester dozes, his face a blank; his harsh lifestyle and abuse of *tzuika*, the ubiquitous liquor distilled from fruit juice, have taken their toll. Lucian, the hunter, is the most talkative. He reckons that about 50 bears still live on the mountains. In his opinion, the loggers should get together and drive the wolves back to Ukraine before they threaten the flocks on isolated farmsteads. In this region, big-game shoots (bear, wolves, deer, chamois, lynx) are sometimes organised for wealthy foreigners willing to fork out a huge sum of money for the chance to bring back a bear weighing about 900 lb (400 kg).

Behind the passenger car clangs a formidable procession of wagons fitted with steel cradles for carrying timber. The train halts before the frail silhouette of a wooden bridge. In this remote valley, the innumerable streams are a steam locomotive's natural allies, and the crew prepare to fill the tender from a rushing torrent. Eventually the agitation of the connecting rods resumes, locomotive noises blending with the gurgling of the stream. A wake of sooty smoke and steam lingers among the pine branches. Meanwhile, more loggers have boarded. The passenger car is full, and the newcomers have to stand in the open timber-wagons, leaning against the cradles and huddled in their sheepskins as the driving snow lashes their faces. They look for all the world like statues being towed by a team of arthritic carthorses.

"We began to drink in the landscape in great gulps, as the trees exploded with snow all around us ..."

Michel Butor *Transit A*

The track follows the course of the River Vaser. Cut into the high sides of the valley are huge channels used by the foresters to roll down the timber. Some of it, however, ends up on the line, and the Mocanitza whistles maniacally to warn the loggers of her approach. Further on, a tree trunk is lying in ambush on a curve, and has to be cleared from the rails. Down below, a man is standing upright in a cart full of logs, furiously whipping the horses as they flounder in the muddy riverbed. Until the 1950s, the timber was taken down the turbulent Vaser on bobbing rafts.

Almost triumphantly, as if of its own accord, the train starts moving again. The scenery that unfolds is awe-inspiring: still, white and hushed beneath the deep snowfall. Beyond the frosted windows of the passenger car, ash striplings flee like a routed army. They give way to pines, ever more numerous, hemming in the track. On the branches accumulated snow and ice form glittering white arches and crystal garlands, shattered by the headlong assault of the engine. Beneath the gusts of smoke and steam a curtain of powdery snow seeks to invade the compartments, while behind the last wagon a mixture of smoke and snowflakes swirls about, glistening like pearl-drops.

Halfway up the incline, the wheels suddenly begin to squeal on the frozen rails, and the asthmatic boiler emits a dreadful gasping. Howls of frustration in the cab. Mircea reduces the steam pressure, which is rising crazily. One of the train crew perches on the narrow ledge overhanging the buffers and grasps the brake handle. Hideous groans of overheated metal. A last shudder, then silence. One of the boiler tubes has given up the ghost. This is not that unusual, and patching it up will take a few hours at most. On the move again, and things get a bit more complicated when tackling a steeper gradient, where a thick fall of snow is beginning to cover the rails. Mircea knows he must reach the little station at Poiana at all costs and fit a snowplough. The firebox is stuffed full to bursting, the pistons battling madly inside the cylinders. A "scalding perspiration", as Théophile Gautier described it, covers the flanks of this old Resita; choking and snorting, she finally runs out of breath. The wheels are sliding; she can go no further, the ice will not yield. Mircea "suggests" that the passengers get off, and everyone joins in clearing the snow. The engine is backed up to allow a run at the obstacle, and after several tries the ice begins to yield. One final, glorious charge and the "forge on wheels" bursts its way up the last few yards of the gradient in an explosion of snow.

Outside Poiana station, a woman, heavily muffled against the cold, serves drinks to loggers carrying axes on their shoulders. The men from the train are here to begin work again, headed for their temporary camp; they will not see their families for another three weeks. Gabril the poet and Lucian the hunter are ready to set off into the forest next morning after wolves. Mircea fusses over every detail as the snowplough is coupled in front of the train. But even with the plough, we will not reach the terminus in the hamlet of Coanaru tonight – there have been too many hitches en route. A "draisine" or railcar – a diesel minibus mounted on a bogie –

ascends the incline with a sort of waddling gait, like a farmyard fowl. Mircea is needed back at the depot and will have to leave his train. A flurry of activity as some of us transfer to the railcar. Lying in the snow, its driver installs a jack under its belly and raises the vehicle, so that the wheels are above the rails. It can now be swivelled round, with the front pointing back down the gradient.

Here, in this isolated valley, strong bonds unite railwaymen with the loggers, whose life is particularly harsh in winter.

The tops of the pine trees are fading into the twilight sky like cathedral spires, while the train pursues its journey far into the night. Watching it pull away, his eyes fixed on the last wreaths of smoke and steam, Mircea wistfully recalls how his family have lived in the Maramures mountains for over 350 years. Why does he evoke with such nostalgia the era of the Habsburgs, the splendours of the Austro-Hungarian Empire, the royal trains? I'm not really sure... "And the train soon disappeared, its white steam mingling with the white of the swirling snow" – Jules Verne *Around the World in Eighty Days*.

With its load of logs, a horse and cart, belonging to another age, descends the Vaser. The loggers are the only inhabitants of the 75,000-acre (30,000-ha) stretch of forest. This isolated valley in the Maramures is inaccessible save by rail.

PRECEDING PAGES: The train stops continually to disembark foresters. Huge, snow-laden pines arch protectively over the track.

Forestry operations (oak, ash, beech, birch and pine), cornerstone of the economy around Viseu de Sus, are linked to the survival of the Mocanitza.

"The whistling, bellowing locomotive ... merged its clamour with that of stream and waterfall, while its smoke twisted in spirals about the dark branches of the pines."

Jules Verne *Around the World in Eighty Days*

"The long comradeship which saw them from one end of the line to the other, jolting along side by side, saying nothing, united by the same toil and the same dangers."

Émile Zola *La Bête humaine*

PRECEDING PAGES:
Ascending the
Vaser valley:
lashed by the
glacial wind,
loggers on the
rattling wagons
cling to the
timber cradles.

TOP AND LEFT:
The ancient
Resita gives up in
mid-ascent, foiled
by the deep snow
and iced rails.
Using tools
carried on board,
Mircea and the
crew couple a
snowplough to
the locomotive.

ABOVE:
Railwayman
coaling the
tender.

ABOVE:
The track must be regularly cleared of trees blown over by the wind or logs rolled down the slopes by the foresters.

RIGHT AND OPPOSITE PAGE:
In winter, these men who work in the valley spend several weeks together in wooden huts, far from their families.

OVERLEAF:
"And the train soon disappeared, its white steam mingling with the white of the swirling snow."
Jules Verne
Around the World in Eighty Days.

	3	4	5	6	7	8	9	10
	13	14	15	16	17	18	19	20
	23	24	25	26	27	28	29	30
	33	34	35	36	37	38	39	40
	43	44	45	46	47	48	49	50
	53	54	55	56	57	58	59	60
	63	64	65	66	67	68	69	70
72	73	74	75	76	77	78	79	80
82	83	84	85	86	87	88	89	90
92	93	94	95	96	97	98	99	100
102	103	104	105	106	107	108	109	110
11	112	113	114	115	116	117	118	119	120
121	122	123	124	125	126	127	128	129	130
131	132	133	134	135	136	137	138	139	140
141	142	143	144	145	146	147	148	149	150
151	152	153	154	155	156	157	158	159	160
161	162	163	164	165	166	167	168	169	170
171	172	173	174	175	176	177	178	189	190
181	182	183	184	185	186	187	188	199	200
191	192	193	194	195	196	197	198	209	210
201	202	203	204	205	206	207	208	219	220
211	212	213	214	215	216	217	218	229	230
221	222	223	224	225	226	227	228	239	240
231	232	233	234	235	236	237	238	249	250
241	242	243	244	245	246	247	248	259	260
251	252	253	254	255	256	257	258	269	270
261	262	263	264	265	266	267	268	279	280
271	272	273	274	275	276	277	278	289	290
281	282	283	284	285	286	287	288	299	300
291	292	293	294	295	296	297	298	309	310
301	302	303	304	305	306	307	308	319	320
311	312	313	314	315	316	317	318	329	330
321	322	323	324	325	326	327	328	339	340
331	332	333	334	335	336	337	338	349	350
341	342	343	344	345	346	347	348	359	360
351	352	353	354	355	356	357	358	369	370
361	362	363	364	365	366	367	368	379	380
371	372	373	374	375	376	377	378	389	390
381	382	383	384	385	386	387	388	399	400
391	392	393	394	395	396	397	398	399	400